Implementing
Juvenile Justice Reform

THE FEDERAL ROLE

Committee on a Prioritized Plan to Implement a Developmental Approach
in Juvenile Justice Reform

Committee on Law and Justice

Division of Behavioral and Social Sciences and Education

NATIONAL RESEARCH COUNCIL
OF THE NATIONAL ACADEMIES

THE NATIONAL ACADEMIES PRESS
Washington, D.C.
www.nap.edu

THE NATIONAL ACADEMIES PRESS　　　**500 Fifth Street, NW**　　　**Washington, DC 20001**

NOTICE: The project that is the subject of this report was approved by the Governing Board of the National Research Council, whose members are drawn from the councils of the National Academy of Sciences, the National Academy of Engineering, and the Institute of Medicine. The members of the committee responsible for the report were chosen for their special competences and with regard for appropriate balance.

This study was supported by Contract No. 2013-JF-FX-K004 from the U.S. Department of Justice/Office of Juvenile Justice and Delinquency Prevention, Contract No. 213.0506 from the Annie E. Casey Foundation, and Contract No. 13-105086-000-USP from the John D. and Catherine T. MacArthur Foundation. Any opinions, findings, conclusions, or recommendations expressed in this publication are those of the author(s) and do not necessarily reflect the views of the organizations or agencies that provided support for the project.

International Standard Book Number-3: 978-0-309-30347-7
International Standard Book Number-0: 0-309-30347-8

Additional copies of this report are available from the National Academies Press, 500 Fifth Street, NW, Keck 360, Washington, DC 20001; (800) 624-6242 or (202) 334-3313; http://www.nap.edu.

Suggested citation: National Research Council. (2014). *Implementing Juvenile Justice Reform: The Federal Role.* Committee on a Prioritized Plan to Implement a Developmental Approach in Juvenile Justice Reform, Committee on Law and Justice, Division of Behavioral and Social Sciences and Education. Washington, DC: The National Academies Press.

THE NATIONAL ACADEMIES
Advisers to the Nation on Science, Engineering, and Medicine

The **National Academy of Sciences** is a private, nonprofit, self-perpetuating society of distinguished scholars engaged in scientific and engineering research, dedicated to the furtherance of science and technology and to their use for the general welfare. Upon the authority of the charter granted to it by the Congress in 1863, the Academy has a mandate that requires it to advise the federal government on scientific and technical matters. Dr. Ralph J. Cicerone is president of the National Academy of Sciences.

The **National Academy of Engineering** was established in 1964, under the charter of the National Academy of Sciences, as a parallel organization of outstanding engineers. It is autonomous in its administration and in the selection of its members, sharing with the National Academy of Sciences the responsibility for advising the federal government. The National Academy of Engineering also sponsors engineering programs aimed at meeting national needs, encourages education and research, and recognizes the superior achievements of engineers. Dr. C. D. Mote, Jr., is president of the National Academy of Engineering.

The **Institute of Medicine** was established in 1970 by the National Academy of Sciences to secure the services of eminent members of appropriate professions in the examination of policy matters pertaining to the health of the public. The Institute acts under the responsibility given to the National Academy of Sciences by its congressional charter to be an adviser to the federal government and, upon its own initiative, to identify issues of medical care, research, and education. Dr. Victor J. Dzau is president of the Institute of Medicine.

The **National Research Council** was organized by the National Academy of Sciences in 1916 to associate the broad community of science and technology with the Academy's purposes of furthering knowledge and advising the federal government. Functioning in accordance with general policies determined by the Academy, the Council has become the principal operating agency of both the National Academy of Sciences and the National Academy of Engineering in providing services to the government, the public, and the scientific and engineering communities. The Council is administered jointly by both Academies and the Institute of Medicine. Dr. Ralph J. Cicerone and Dr. C. D. Mote, Jr., are chair and vice chair, respectively, of the National Research Council.

www.nationalacademies.org

Preface

In 2013, *Reforming Juvenile Justice: A Development Approach* was published by the National Research Council (NRC). In that report, a committee charged with assessing recent initiatives in juvenile justice strongly endorsed a framework of reform based on a scientific understanding of adolescent development. The report was well received within the juvenile justice community and by policy makers in states, localities, and tribal jurisdictions, as well as within the Department of Justice. Many of us who participated on the committee that produced *Reforming Juvenile Justice* detected a sense of urgency about moving forward after the report was published: "This moment should not be lost," we were advised.

In this context, we were pleased that the newly appointed administrator of the Office of Juvenile Justice and Delinquency Prevention (OJJDP) initiated a dialogue with the NRC about the possibility of a follow-up study to develop an implementation plan for OJJDP. With the help of the Annie E. Casey Foundation and the John D. and Catherine T. MacArthur Foundation, the project was funded in late 2013 and an expedited study began soon thereafter. This report, the product of that study, is designed to provide specific guidance to OJJDP regarding the steps that it should take, both internally and externally, to facilitate juvenile justice reform grounded in knowledge about adolescent development.

As this report explains, the plan is ambitious and OJJDP will need to overcome many impediments in order to achieve it. However, the committee is confident that this plan can be carried out successfully by building on past efforts of OJJDP and current reforms under way in many states—especially if the agency has the political and material support it will need from Congress and the U.S. Department of Justice. It is important for leaders in the Department of Justice and on relevant congressional committees to understand that juvenile justice reform should be seen as a priority for improving the nation's justice system as well as a key element of the nation's youth policy.

The committee notes that this report offers, as requested by the OJJDP administrator, an itemized plan of action over the next 3 years, and we applaud the agency's sense of urgency. We have proposed a 3-year plan because the committee shares the view that we are at a critical moment in juvenile justice reform. Responsibility for propelling juvenile justice reform forward and for sustaining it in the coming decades is the right and appropriate role for the federal government through OJJDP. This must not be seen as a transient priority. It must be seen by Congress and future attorneys general as the preeminent mission for the agency under the Juvenile Justice and Delinquency Prevention Act.

I wish to express my deep appreciation to the members of the committee for their diligent and dedicated contributions to this study and to the preparation of this report within an expedited time frame. The diverse expertise and experience offered by each member of the committee were indispensable to the formulation of the "prioritized plan" incorporated in this report for implementing a developmental approach in juvenile justice reform.

Richard J. Bonnie, *Chair*
Committee on a Prioritized Plan to Implement a
Developmental Approach in Juvenile Justice Reform

Acknowledgments

This report has been reviewed in draft form by individuals chosen for their diverse perspectives and technical expertise, in accordance with procedures approved by the National Research Council's (NRC's) Report Review Committee. The purpose of this independent review is to provide candid and critical comments that will assist the institution in making its published report as sound as possible and to ensure that the report meets institutional standards for objectivity, evidence, and responsiveness to the study charge. The review comments and draft manuscript remain confidential to protect the integrity of the deliberative process. We wish to thank the following individuals for their review of this report: Eugene Bardach, Goldman School of Public Policy, University of California; Shay Bilchik, Juvenile Justice Reform, McCourt School of Public Policy, Georgetown University; Karen S. Cook, Department of Sociology, Stanford University; Hermann Habermann, independent consultant, Arlington, VA; Ned Loughran, Council of Juvenile Correctional Administrators, Braintree, MA; George D. Mosee, Jr., Juvenile Division, Philadelphia, PA; Daniel S. Nagin, H.J. Heinz School of Public Policy, Carnegie Mellon University; Julie J. Ryan, Engineering Management and Systems Engineering, George Washington University; Marc A. Schindler, Executive Director's Office, Justice Policy Institute, Washington, DC; Lawrence D. Steinberg, Department of Psychology, Temple University; Juliana Stratton, Executive Director's Office, Cook County Justice Advisory Council, Chicago, IL; and Joshua Weber, Juvenile Justice, Council of State Governments Justice Center, Bethesda, MD.

Although the reviewers listed above have provided many constructive comments and suggestions, they were not asked to endorse the conclusions or recommendations nor did they see the final draft of the report before its release. The review of this report was overseen by the monitor, Charles F. Manski (National Academy of Sciences), board of trustees professor of economics, Department of Economics, Northwestern University, and coordinator John E. Rolph, professor emeritus of statistics, University of Southern California. Appointed by the NRC, they were responsible for making certain that an independent examination of this report was carried out in accordance with institutional procedures and that all review comments were carefully considered. Responsibility for the final content of this report rests entirely with the authoring committee and the institution.

The committee is grateful to the staff of OJJDP as well as the representatives of the Annie E. Casey Foundation and the John D. and Catherine T. MacArthur Foundation for their active participation throughout the study. The committee also recognizes Cheryl Hayes for providing an assessment of the current federal budget to identify funding streams that may be used to support activities for youths involved in the juvenile justice system, and John Wilson, who served as a consultant to the committee, for bringing his wisdom and expertise from 30 years of experience at OJJDP to bear on the study. The committee applauds the NRC staff members—Arlene Lee, Daniel Talmage, Julie Schuck, and Emily Backes—for their dedication to the study and to the preparation of this report. We would also like to thank Mary Ghitelman for her administrative support throughout the study process. And finally we thank the executive office reports staff of the Division of Behavioral and Social Sciences and Education, especially Robert Katt (consultant editor), who provided valuable help with editing the report, and Kirsten Sampson Snyder, who managed the report review process. Without the NRC's guidance and wise counsel, the committee's job would have been even more difficult if not impossible.

Contents

APPENDIXES

Figures, Tables, and Boxes

Acronyms and Abbreviations

ABA   American Bar Association

BJA   Bureau of Justice Assistance

CIT   Crisis Intervention Team
CJJ   Coalition for Juvenile Justice
COPS   Community Oriented Policing Services

DOJ   U.S. Department of Justice

FACJJ   Federal Advisory Committee on Juvenile Justice

GAO   U.S. Government Accountability Office

IACP   International Association of Chiefs of Police
IJA   Institute of Judicial Administration

JABG   Juvenile Accountability Block Grant
JJDPA   Juvenile Justice and Delinquency Prevention Act of 1974

NIC   National Institute of Corrections
NRC   National Research Council
NYCDOP   New York City Department of Probation

OJJDP   Office of Juvenile Justice and Delinquency Prevention
OJP   Office of Justice Programs

SAG   State Advisory Group
SAMHSA   Substance Abuse and Mental Health Services Administration

TTA   training and technical assistance

Summary

In the past decade, a number of state, local, and tribal jurisdictions have taken significant steps to improve their juvenile justice systems—for example, reducing the use of juvenile detention and out-of-home placement, using assessment tools to identify risks and needs, bringing greater attention to racial and ethnic disparities, looking for ways to engage affected families in the process, and raising the age at which juvenile court jurisdiction ends. These changes reflect heightening awareness of the ineffectiveness of punitive practices and accumulating knowledge about the implications of adolescent development for reforming the juvenile justice system. Momentum for reform is growing. However, many more state, local, and tribal jurisdictions need assistance, and practitioners in the juvenile justice field are looking for guidance from the federal government, particularly from the Office of Juvenile Justice and Delinquency Prevention (OJJDP) in the U.S. Department of Justice (DOJ) as the sole agency charged with addressing juvenile delinquency.

In 2013, the National Research Council (NRC) published a report, *Reforming Juvenile Justice: A Developmental Approach* (hereafter, the 2013 NRC report), which consolidated the research on adolescent development and the effects of justice system interventions and summarized the state of current reform efforts. That report shows how knowledge about adolescent development aligns with the goals of the juvenile justice system (holding youths accountable, being fair, and preventing reoffending). Taking a "developmental approach" to juvenile justice was seen as embracing policies and practices at every decision point, and by every actor or participant, that are informed by, and compatible with, evolving knowledge about adolescent development and with research evidence on the effects of juvenile justice interventions.

The 2013 NRC report made four broad recommendations based on the research findings and on the central idea that a developmental approach should guide juvenile justice system improvement: (1) state and tribal governments should create oversight bodies to design, implement, and oversee a long-term process of juvenile justice reform; (2) OJJDP should assume a strengthened federal role, to support juvenile justice system improvement; (3) federal agencies should support research to advance the science of adolescent development and improve understanding of effective responses to delinquency; and (4) OJJDP should guide a data improvement program. The report emphasized that laws, policies, and practices at every stage within the system should align with the evolving knowledge of adolescent development (National Research Council, 2013, pp. 1-14).

After the release of the 2013 report, the NRC appointed the Committee on a Prioritized Plan to Implement a Developmental Approach in Juvenile Justice Reform to identify and prioritize federal strategies and policies to effectively facilitate reform of the juvenile justice system and develop an implementation plan for OJJDP (see statement of task in Chapter 1). This report lays out that plan and recommendations, including proposals regarding the agency's priorities, budget, and operations. Although the committee recognizes that OJJDP has other responsibilities, the report focuses on juvenile justice system improvement in response to its charge as well as the growing demand for leadership and change within juvenile justice.

OJJDP has been widely viewed in recent years as being in a state of limited capacity and stature. The agency has not been reauthorized since 2002. Appropriated funding has declined by half in current dollars since 2003-2010, but more importantly the discretion that OJJDP has to use its funding has been sharply compromised. Directed priorities from Congress and the Department of Justice have undercut OJJDP's ability to assist states and localities with juvenile justice system issues and improvements and with delinquency prevention programs targeting youths most at risk of system involvement. At this time, OJJDP's program portfolio focuses heavily on preventive interventions that target children well before any indication of likely involvement with the justice system. As a result, OJJDP's portfolio needs to be rebalanced. The 2013 NRC report emphasized that the juvenile justice system is in critical need of assistance, and OJJDP is the only federal agency specifically mandated to provide assistance to this system. This committee, like the committee that authored the 2013 NRC report, acknowledges that OJJDP's authorizing legislation, the Juvenile Justice and Delinquency Prevention Act, as amended (P.L. 107-273; JJDPA), provides the agency with the appropriate authority and functions to be a leader in juvenile justice reform. However, that authority and OJJDP's capacity to focus on system reform need to be strengthened.

This report identifies seven hallmarks of a developmental approach to juvenile justice. A developmental approach puts into practice what we know from research on adolescent development and on the effectiveness of juvenile justice interventions. These hallmarks provide a template to guide system reform:

1. Accountability Without Criminalization
2. Alternatives to Justice System Involvement
3. Individualized Response Based on Assessment of Needs and Risks
4. Confinement Only When Necessary for Public Safety
5. A Genuine Commitment to Fairness
6. Sensitivity to Disparate Treatment
7. Family Engagement

The report outlines how these hallmarks of a developmental approach should be incorporated into policies and practices within OJJDP, as well as in actions taken by state, local, and tribal jurisdictions to achieve the goals of the juvenile justice system.[1]

Most of the steps recommended in this report can be accomplished under the current statutory framework of the JJDPA, and much of what is recommended can be effectuated even within the agency's limited funding capacity—if the agency is creative in using the flexibility allowed by available funding streams and in leveraging other sources of support. However, OJJDP's ability to effect change in the juvenile justice field in the foreseeable future will be severely constrained without adequate legislative and budgetary support by federal policy makers. Therefore, although most of the committee's recommendations below[2] are directed at OJJDP, the committee also urges federal policy makers to demonstrate support for a developmental approach to juvenile justice and delinquency prevention and to bolster OJJDP's capacity to lead and facilitate system reform.

SUPPORT BY FEDERAL POLICY MAKERS FOR IMPROVING THE JUVENILE JUSTICE SYSTEM

Reauthorization of the JJDPA will establish a firm foundation for OJJDP's role in the transformative work ahead, as well as signaling to the field that the nation has entered the next stage in juvenile justice reform based upon the research and science of adolescent development. The reauthorizing legislation, if adopted, should under-

---

[1] The goals or aims of the juvenile courts and affiliated agencies of the juvenile justice system have been expressed as follows: holding youths accountable for wrongdoing, preventing further offending, and treating juveniles fairly (National Research Council, 2013, p.10).

[2] Note that the numbering of the recommendations reflects their placement as developed in the chapters of this report.

score federal support for juvenile justice system improvements based on the science of adolescent development and on scientific evidence regarding the effects of justice system interventions. Reauthorization of JJDPA with strengthened legislative language would send a strong message regarding the need for state, local, and tribal governments to assume greater responsibility for administering a developmentally appropriate juvenile justice system as a condition for federal support.

OJJDP's ability to effect change in the juvenile justice field in the foreseeable future will be severely constrained without adequate legislative and budgetary support by federal policy makers. When OJJDP is reauthorized, it should be directed, as recommended by the 2013 NRC report, to base its programs and activities on the scientific knowledge regarding adolescent development and the effects of delinquency prevention programs and juvenile justice interventions; to link state plans and training of state advisory groups to the accumulating knowledge about adolescent development; to modify the definitions for "status offenses" and for an "adult inmate" so that all adolescents are treated appropriately; and to identify support for developmentally informed juvenile justice system improvement as one of the agency's responsibilities.

OJJDP continues to be assigned responsibility for programs that do not directly involve the juvenile justice system or youths connected with the justice system. Funds for these programs have been carved out of OJJDP's shrinking total budget through appropriations. As a result of a declining source of discretionary funds, OJJDP's capacity to help improve the juvenile justice system has been materially diminished. One of the key recommendations in the 2013 NRC report was that federal policy makers should restore OJJDP's capacity to carry out its mission through reauthorization, appropriations, and funding flexibility (National Research Council, 2013, p. 328; reproduced in Box 3-2 of this report).

To realize greater impact, it may be necessary to further target appropriations on reform of the juvenile justice system. Even if the agency is given greater flexibility in using its funding, its current appropriations do not give it adequate capacity to conduct the activities that were envisioned by Congress in enacting the JJDPA in 1974 or to carry out the vision articulated in this report. The main solution to that problem is to assure that the agency has the necessary resources for staffing, grants, training, and technical assistance.

OJJDP's ability to carry out its mission requires adequate legislative and budgetary support by federal policy makers. Assisting states, localities, and tribal jurisdictions to align their juvenile justice systems and delinquency prevention programs with current best practices and the results of research on adolescent development and implementing developmentally informed policies, programs, and practices should be the agency's top priority under the JJDPA. Any additional responsibilities and authority conferred on the agency should be amply funded so as not to erode the funds needed to carry out support for system improvement. The funds available to OJJDP need to be ample enough, and sufficiently flexible, to enable the agency to hire, train, and retain the necessary staff and to provide the demonstration grants, research, and technical assistance needed to support developmentally informed justice system improvements and reforms by states, tribes, and localities.

While OJJDP is the federal agency designated to improve the juvenile justice system, it is one of many agencies within DOJ. Implementation of a developmental approach to juvenile justice will require the support and leadership of the Office of Justice Programs and DOJ. Acceptance and formal recognition of the hallmarks of a developmental approach to juvenile justice reform across DOJ agencies is a necessary condition for carrying out the strategy outlined in this report.

Recommendation 5-1: The U.S. Department of Justice, including but not limited to the Office of Justice Programs, should authorize, publicly support, and actively partner with OJJDP to provide federal support for developmentally oriented juvenile justice reform in states, localities, and tribal jurisdictions. The federal initiative should include strategic training and technical assistance; demonstration programs; and a range of incentives to states, localities, and tribes to achieve specific outcomes for justice-involved youths, as well as specific system changes.

OJJDP'S LEADERSHIP ROLE

This report provides an implementation plan for OJJDP.[3] The agency has a broad mandate with responsibilities to provide assistance and support research across the continuum of delinquency prevention and justice system interventions. OJJDP should use all of the tools at its disposal to support reform efforts: dispensing formula and block grants, providing training and technical assistance, funding demonstration programs, supporting research and data collection, and disseminating information. OJJDP will need to rebalance its activities and programs and fortify its internal capacity to administer them through intensive staff training. OJJDP should also ensure that all stakeholders and participants in the juvenile justice system are trained appropriately and understand the hallmarks of a developmental approach. In a parallel and continuous research agenda, OJJDP should gather data, measure progress, synthesize lessons learned, and facilitate iterative improvements as it points the way toward a juvenile justice system that is fair, holds youths accountable in a developmentally appropriate manner, and prevents re-offending.

Building Internal Capacity

OJJDP will need to incorporate the hallmarks of a developmental approach in all of its operations, including training and technical assistance, research, demonstration programs, and partnerships. This will require a concerted effort to realign the organizational culture with the new vision. OJJDP should strive to ensure that each of its divisions is well staffed with trained professionals knowledgeable about the science of adolescent development and skilled in the areas needed to guide a strategic reform effort based on a developmental approach.

Recommendation 3-1: OJJDP should develop a staff training curriculum based on the hallmarks of a developmental approach to juvenile justice reform. With the assistance of a team of external experts, it should implement the training curriculum on an ongoing basis and train, assign, or hire staff to align its capabilities with the skills and expertise needed to carry out a developmentally oriented approach to juvenile justice reform.

Based on perceptions in the field, as well as personnel assignments, it appears that OJJDP's operations are burdened by grant monitoring tasks for both the general monitoring of all its grants and the enforcement of compliance with the core protections stipulated by the JJDPA (despite high rates of compliance with those protections). While ensuring that awarded monies are used appropriately is imperative, the committee is convinced that this function can be reconfigured so as to redirect staffing resources toward system reform efforts. OJJDP should re-examine the monitoring systems and revisit past approaches by the agency to identify ways to ensure compliance that is less resource-intensive, such as a system of random audits, a rotating schedule of full reviews, or contracting out the monitoring function.

Recommendation 3-2: OJJDP should establish a better balance between grant monitoring and system reform efforts by examining more efficient ways to monitor grants and compliance with the core protections from the JJDPA.

Facilitating Reform

Leadership of reform within the states may come from a variety of places, depending upon the state, local, or tribal jurisdiction: grassroots advocates, change agent leaders, or policy makers. A potentially critical role in promoting state-level reforms can be played by State Advisory Groups (SAGs), which are composed of citizens,

---

[3]In addition to the formal recommendations to OJJDP developed in Chapters 3 through 5 and noted in this Summary, the implementation plan also includes, in Chapter 6, specific action steps for implementing the recommendations. The action steps are set out over a 3-year period to provide OJJDP and the Department of Justice with a detailed temporal roadmap for implementing reform of the juvenile justice system using a developmentally informed approach.

advocates, and government officials at various levels. The SAGs serve several functions, including overseeing juvenile justice grant funds from OJJDP, monitoring the four core-protection requirements, and developing or reviewing a 3-year state plan. They therefore have the potential to become key players in juvenile justice reform, serving as one of the leaders for reform efforts that OJJDP could leverage at the state level.

Recommendation 4-1: OJJDP should promote the development and strengthening of the State Advisory Groups (SAGs) to be juvenile justice reform leaders by supporting meaningful family and youth engagement, fostering partnerships, delivering strategic training and technical assistance aimed at facilitating reform, and ensuring that SAG members and staff are knowledgeable about the hallmarks of a developmental approach to juvenile justice.

The committee has conceived a technical assistance framework that provides capacity-building support to state, local, and tribal jurisdictions, including the SAGs, in two broad categories: tactical and strategic. Tactical forms of technical assistance are specific and short in duration, such as the development of a risk assessment tool and training on its use. Strategic technical assistance is more comprehensive, provided over a long time horizon, and better suited for addressing complex issues. Strategic technical assistance spans multiple years, and when it is well executed, it is customized to the local level and decisions are guided by data. Both strategic and tactical technical assistance are tools necessary for OJJDP to guide reform. Given the expense of a long-term commitment of technical assistance and the scarcity of resources, OJJDP must be strategic in deciding which localities or states are eligible to receive the assistance, under what specific circumstances, and through which carefully selected providers that have demonstrated expertise in adolescent development.

Recommendation 4-2: OJJDP should develop a portfolio of training and technical assistance, properly balanced to be both strategic and tactical, to support the implementation of a developmental approach to juvenile justice reform. OJJDP should coordinate with agencies and organizations proficient in providing training and technical assistance based on the hallmarks of a developmental approach to juvenile justice reform. This proficiency should include historical experience working in system improvement efforts.

Recommendation 4-3: All applicants for technical assistance or demonstration grants sponsored by OJJDP should be required to show how they would use the assistance, either strategically or tactically, to implement or strengthen a developmental approach to juvenile justice reform.

Recommendation 5-7: OJJDP should increase its capacity to provide training and technical assistance by initiating or capitalizing on partnerships with national organizations that provide training and guidance to their membership and recognize the need for enhanced training in the hallmarks of a developmental approach to juvenile justice reform.

With its existing statutory authority, OJJDP could develop a multiyear pilot program for jurisdictions demonstrating readiness to develop a developmentally appropriate system that promotes accountability, ensures fairness with attention to reducing racial and ethnic disparities, and reduces the risk of further delinquency. Selected jurisdictions can demonstrate this readiness through, for instance, a willingness to measure youth outcomes and system improvement progress over time; fostering partnerships; and identifying avenues for participation of system-involved youths and families in the development of policies, practices, and programs. The selected sites could be viewed from the outset as "learning laboratories" that provide guidance to new jurisdictions as OJJDP takes the effort to scale.

Recommendation 4-5: In partnership with other federal agencies and the philanthropic community, OJJDP should develop a multiyear demonstration project designed to provide substantial technical assistance and financial support to selected states and localities to develop a comprehensive plan for reforming the state's juvenile justice system based on a developmental approach. The demonstration grant should include a

requirement for strategies that reduce racial and ethnic disparities and the unnecessary use of confinement as well as other hallmarks of a developmental approach. OJJDP should ensure that State Advisory Group (SAG) members in states with demonstration sites are intimately involved in their state's pilot projects and help disseminate lessons learned to other states' SAGs.

Reducing Racial and Ethnic Disparities

Reducing racial and ethnic disparities is a critical element of juvenile justice reform. Whatever their underlying causes, continued disparities call into question the fairness of the juvenile justice system (National Research Council, 2013, p. 211). They also reinforce social disaffection and disrespect for law among minority youths at a developmentally sensitive time (National Research Council, 2013, p. 194). While reducing racial and ethnic disparities has been a focus of the OJJDP for more than a decade, little progress has been made toward this goal—due in part to various combinations of lack of incentives, lack of cross-system collaboration, inadequate resources, the extreme difficulties of disentangling the many complex contributing factors, and deeply embedded structural biases.

OJJDP's current approach to the disproportionate minority contact provision in the JJDPA, focusing on the collection of Relative Rate Index data from states, has not been effective. New guidelines should be developed that require each jurisdiction to identify specific decision points where disparities emerge or are magnified, assess the reasons for these disparities, develop a plan for modifying the policy or practice that appears to be producing the disparities, evaluate outcomes of the plan, and revise and improve the plan if necessary to reduce disparities. In addition, OJJDP can help promote a fairer and more equitable system, and therefore a more developmentally appropriate system, by highlighting promising practices in reducing disparities and providing meaningful and well-informed training and technical assistance to the field, including peer learning opportunities. The committee is confident that OJJDP has authority to adopt this approach without any change in the JJDPA.

Recommendation 4-4: OJJDP should establish new approaches for identifying racial and ethnic disparities across the juvenile justice system, promulgate new guidelines for reducing and eliminating racial and ethnic disparities, build the internal capacity and/or establish partnerships for assisting states with these new requirements, and strengthen the role of State Advisory Groups (SAGs) in monitoring the new guidelines by providing training and technical assistance to SAGs.

Creating Strategic Partnerships

Developing strategic partnerships will be critical for achieving system reform. OJJDP will have to not only strengthen or develop partnerships at the federal level but also facilitate partnerships within the jurisdictions and among stakeholder groups. The committee believes OJJDP should focus on those partnerships that will have the greatest impact on the goal of achieving a more developmentally appropriate juvenile justice system. In the short term, partnerships should help the agency implement the recommendations and action items in this report, such as developing and executing a training curriculum, designing a demonstration grant program, and identifying strategic opportunities to support an innovative reform. Over the longer term, partnerships should be designed to help monitor, replicate, and sustain system reforms.

Recommendation 5-2: OJJDP should initiate and support collaborative partnerships at the federal, state, local, and tribal levels and should use them strategically to advance the goal of a developmentally appropriate juvenile justice system.

The JJDPA authorizes an independent Coordinating Council on Juvenile Justice and Delinquency Prevention, whose purpose is to coordinate relevant federal work and to support state and local juvenile justice programs. While the recent impact and role of this council has been unclear and funding to support its work has declined substantially, the coordinating council provides an established structure through which OJJDP can lead and coordinate an initiative with federal partners assigned to the council and can fully engage system-involved youths and families at the federal level by including their perspective in guiding policy, practice, and reform.

Recommendation 5-3: OJJDP should establish and convene, on an ongoing basis, a Family Advisory Group to the Coordinating Council on Juvenile Justice and Delinquency Prevention, composed of youths and families whose lives have been impacted by the juvenile justice system.

Recommendation 5-4: OJJDP, with the support of the attorney general, should use the Coordinating Council on Juvenile Justice and Delinquency Prevention strategically to implement key components of developmentally oriented juvenile justice reform through interagency, intergovernmental (federal-state-local partnering), and public-private partnering activities with specific measurable objectives.

Preventing and reducing delinquent behavior requires the collective knowledge and resources of the members of this coordinating council along with other federal agencies. While OJJDP is the only federal agency specifically authorized to improve the juvenile justice system, it is not the only agency that has the ability to contribute to this mission. Durable, long-term, systemic improvements that result in improved outcomes for youths in the juvenile justice system depend on the coordination of categorical funding from health, behavioral health, social services, education, juvenile justice, housing, and workforce development.

Recommendation 5-5: OJJDP should work with its federal agency and Coordinating Council on Juvenile Justice and Delinquency Prevention partners (i) to blend or leverage available federal funds to support OJJDP demonstration projects and (ii) to provide guidance to eligible grantees on leveraging federal funding at the state or local level.

It has been almost 35 years since the American Bar Association (ABA) approved the *Juvenile Justice Standards*. Review and reconsideration of the standards is long overdue in light of developments in the law as well as advances in knowledge about adolescent development. The committee understands that the ABA's Criminal Justice Section Executive Committee is considering initiation of a process to review and revise the existing *Juvenile Justice Standards*. The committee hopes that the ABA will undertake this project and that it will convene a multidisciplinary task force to conduct the necessary study, with participation by the relevant professional, scientific, and stakeholder organizations. If the ABA does decide to undertake this project, the Department of Justice, acting through OJJDP, should participate actively and provide its full support.

Recommendation 5-6: OJJDP, with support of the attorney general, should support and participate in an American Bar Association project to formulate a new and updated volume of standards for juvenile justice based on the developmental approach.

Building the Statistical Foundation to Assess Reform

Currently, many jurisdictions develop their own information management systems or contract with businesses to develop such systems, largely de novo. This makes generalizable knowledge and collaborative problem solving difficult. Attaining an acceptable level of uniformity in administrative data collection across states and localities would make cross-site comparisons and projects possible. OJJDP is the only agency that is positioned to promote the needed consistency across data systems in the various jurisdictions.

Recommendation 3-3: OJJDP should take a leadership role in local, state, and tribal jurisdictions with respect to the development and implementation of administrative data systems by providing model formats for system structure, standards, and common definitions of data elements. OJJDP should also provide consultation on data systems as well as opportunities for sharing information across jurisdictions.

Since its establishment, OJJDP has promoted research and data collection. The research programs it has supported have focused on collecting and analyzing information on numbers of juveniles at various stages of the system, on identifying individual programs that "work" to prevent or reduce delinquency among the program participants (measured almost exclusively by re-arrest rates), and on identifying factors related to the development or continuation of delinquency. Although these efforts continue to be useful, data collection and research are needed to identify and measure the effects of particular juvenile justice practices or policies on adolescent development and to understand developmental influences on the effectiveness of juvenile justice practices and policies.

Recommendation 3-4: OJJDP should focus research efforts toward specific projects related to a developmental perspective on juvenile justice, capitalizing on an integration of its research and program efforts.

CONCLUSION

Reform of the nation's juvenile justice systems grounded in advancing knowledge about adolescent development is a widely supported goal, crossing the usual lines of political disagreement. The 2013 NRC report summarized the scientific foundation for a developmental approach and distilled its implications for reform. This new report sets forth a detailed and prioritized strategic plan for the federal government to support and facilitate a developmental approach to juvenile justice reform. The pivotal component of the plan is to strengthen the role, capacity, and commitment of OJJDP, the lead federal agency in the field. By carrying out the recommendations in this report, the federal government will both reaffirm and advance the promise of the Juvenile Justice and Delinquency Prevention Act.

1

Introduction

A movement is under way to change the treatment of youths in the nation's juvenile justice system based on accumulating knowledge about adolescent development and the effects of justice system interventions. Public officials in states and localities are taking steps to reform their juvenile justice systems, supported by an impressive array of foundations, national organizations, and academic institutions. A consensus is emerging that the correctional model of juvenile justice should be replaced by a developmentally oriented approach that keeps youths in their communities, avoids formal legal involvement unless necessary to ensure accountability or protect public safety, and provides whatever services and interventions are needed to support the prosocial development of youths whose cases are diverted from or referred to the juvenile justice system for formal processing. Policy makers and practitioners have also expressed increasing interest in evidence about "what works" for justice-involved youths. The National Research Council report *Reforming Juvenile Justice: A Developmental Approach* was published in 2013 (hereafter, the 2013 NRC report) to consolidate in one volume the results of research on adolescent development and on the effects of justice system interventions and to summarize and assess recent reforms. This report draws on the findings and conclusions of the 2013 NRC report to examine how the federal government can best support reform efforts in the states and localities.

The Office of Juvenile Justice and Delinquency Prevention (OJJDP) was established in 1974 under the Juvenile Justice and Delinquency Prevention Act (JJDPA) (P.L. 93-415, 42 U.S.C. §5601 *et seq*) and authorized to assist state, local, and tribal jurisdictions in their efforts to improve their juvenile justice systems. The agency's early authorizing legislation recognized, as a guiding premise, that juvenile offenders should be treated differently from adults and should receive individualized services in a developmentally appropriate setting. The agency is housed within the U.S. Department of Justice (DOJ) in the Office of Justice Programs. Unlike most federal agencies, OJJDP has a broad mandate with responsibilities that include collecting and documenting data on juveniles in the system; providing support for state, tribal, and local program development; funding research and evaluation, information dissemination, training, and technical assistance; and ensuring compliance with core protections established for states participating in the formula grants program of the JJDPA. This range of functions from supporting research to providing assistance has allowed OJJDP over the years to develop a unique research-to-practice continuum in which its research portfolio is focused on practitioners' needs, using research knowledge and statistics to inform its program development (National Research Council, 2013). In addition, the breadth of OJJDP's mission from delinquency prevention to juvenile justice system interventions allows the agency to be holistic in its approach to addressing issues facing the practitioners in the juvenile justice field (Bilchik, 2010, cited in National Research Council, 2013).

THE CHANGING LANDSCAPE OF JUVENILE JUSTICE

During the 1980s and 1990s, juvenile justice systems across the country were reshaped to embrace a correctional model, relying heavily on placing youths adjudicated as delinquent in facilities outside their homes and communities. The national confinement rate of juveniles rose steadily from 167 per 100,000 population in 1979 to 221 in 1989, reaching a peak in 1997 of 356 juveniles in out-of-home placement[1] per 100,000 population before starting to decline (Allen-Hagen, 1991; Child Trends, n.d.; Kline, 1989; Office of Juvenile Justice and Delinquency Prevention, 1983; Sickmund et al., 2011). In addition, the total number of juveniles held in adult jails rose dramatically from 1,736 nationally in 1983 to 8,090 in 1998, a 366 percent increase. In the late 1990s, 13 percent of confined juveniles were in adult jails or prisons (Austin et al., 2000).

In many cases, confining youths away from their homes and communities interferes with the social conditions that contribute to adolescents' healthy psychological development: the presence of an involved parent or parent figure, association with prosocial peers, and activities that require autonomous decision making and critical thinking (National Research Council, 2013). Many families are torn apart by increased mental, emotional, and financial strain through the processes of juvenile justice system involvement. In addition, family members are often excluded from decisions on the treatment of the children (Justice for Families, 2012). As youths enter adulthood, they can face collateral consequences of involvement in the justice system, such as the public release of juvenile and criminal records that follow them throughout their lives and limit future education and employment opportunities (National Research Council, 2013).

Another controversial trend in the late 1980s and early 1990s was an increase in the number of juveniles prosecuted in adult criminal courts. According to OJJDP, juvenile cases transferred to adult criminal courts via judicial waiver peaked in 1994 at 13,300 cases, two times greater than the number in 1985. However, this figure substantially understates the number of juveniles prosecuted in criminal courts; it does not include many youths whose cases initiated in the criminal courts at the outset, either because (1) youths were older than the jurisdictional age of juvenile court in states that established criminal court jurisdiction at age 16 or 17, or (2) state laws specifically established jurisdiction for the offense in the adult criminal court and excluded it from original juvenile court jurisdiction, or (3) prosecutors had the authority to file the case directly in the criminal court due to the nature of the charge (Puzzanchera and Addie, 2014). Many states redrew the jurisdictional boundaries of the juvenile and criminal courts during this period, excluding certain offenses from juvenile court jurisdiction or authorizing prosecutors to "direct file"[2] many more cases in criminal court. As a result of these developments, the number of juveniles sentenced to lengthy periods of confinement as criminal offenders in adult facilities increased substantially (Austin et al., 2000; Puzzanchera and Addie, 2014).

Youths prosecuted in the adult criminal justice system fare worse than those who remain in the juvenile justice system. According to the 2013 NRC report, ". . . adolescents are in a formative developmental stage in which their social context is likely to shape the trajectory of their future lives" (National Research Council, 2013, p. 135). In adult prisons, youths are more likely to experience victimization, isolation, interaction with adults who seem unconcerned for their welfare, and insufficient educational and therapeutic programs—none of which is likely to reduce recidivism and may in fact increase re-offending and contribute to additional developmental harm (American Academy of Child and Adolescent Psychiatry, 2012; Austin et al., 2000; Beck et al., 1993; Bishop and Frazier, 2000; Forst et al., 1989; Redding, 2008; Task Force on Community Preventive Services, 2007).

These disadvantages are borne disproportionately by minority youths, who are overrepresented at every stage of the juvenile justice process and remain in the system longer than white youths do (National Council on Crime

---

[1]Rates are calculated per 100,000 juveniles ages 10 through the upper age limit of each state's original juvenile court jurisdiction (Child Trends, n.d.; Sickmund et al., 2011).

[2]Statutes in 15 states define a category of cases in which the prosecutor may determine whether to proceed initially in juvenile or criminal court. Typically, these direct-file provisions give both juvenile and adult criminal courts the power to hear cases involving certain offenses or age/offense categories, leaving it up to the prosecutor to make discretionary decisions about where to file them. Of course, prosecutors often have considerable discretionary powers in this area even in the absence of formal statutory authority. In their charging decisions, for instance, they may sometimes, in effect, choose the forum in which the case will be heard. What distinguishes direct-file authority is that it rests on the juvenile and criminal courts' concurrent jurisdiction over a given type of case. Available: http://www.ojjdp.gov/pubs/tryingjuvasadult/transfer2.html [August 2014].

and Delinquency, 2007; Puzzanchera and Adams, 2011; Sickmund et al., 2011). Racial disparities within the juvenile justice system raise at least two types of concerns. First, they call into question the overall fairness and legitimacy of the juvenile justice system. Second, they have serious implications for the life-course trajectories of many justice-involved minority youths who may be traumatized, stigmatized, and adversely affected in other ways by criminal records attained at comparatively young ages (National Research Council, 2013).

Despite a research and policy focus on this matter for more than two decades, remarkably little progress has been made toward reducing the disparities themselves. However, at least in the past decade, some jurisdictions have begun to take significant steps to overhaul their juvenile justice systems in ways that are intended to reduce involvement of minority youths in the system, reduce the use of punitive practices, and heighten awareness of racial disparities (for more discussion, see the 2013 NRC report, Chapter 8, pp. 211-240).

In recent years, a significant number of jurisdictions have taken steps to reduce the use of juvenile detention and out-of-home placement. From 1997 to 2010, such confinement declined as much as 65 percent in some states (Sickmund et al., 2011). By 2010, the national confinement rate of juveniles in the juvenile justice system was down to 225 per 100,000 population (Child Trends, n.d.; Sickmund et al., 2011).

The complex statutes governing the jurisdictional boundary between juvenile and criminal court prosecutions are also being modified in many jurisdictions to keep more adolescents in juvenile court. For example, an increasing number of states are raising the age of juvenile court jurisdiction to its traditional line at 18; as of 2013, 40 states designate 18 as the maximum age of original juvenile court jurisdiction (Butts and Roman, 2014). The U.S. Supreme Court has noted the developmental basis for these ameliorative reforms in a series of recent decisions forbidding the most severe penalties, most notably the death penalty and sentences of life in prison without parole, for offenders younger than 18 (*Graham v. Florida*, 2010; *Miller v. Alabama*, 2012; National Research Council, 2013, p. 43-44; *Roper v. Simmons,* 2005).

Momentum for juvenile justice reform is growing, but the necessary institutional changes have not occurred in many parts of the country. According to the 2013 NRC report (pp. 3-4):

> Substantial progress has been made by various states and local jurisdictions in embracing and implementing a more developmentally appropriate way of handling youth who come to the attention of the juvenile justice system. However, when viewed nationally, the pace of reform has been sluggish. Many changes that have occurred have not been evaluated in a sufficiently rigorous and systematic manner to enable other reform-minded jurisdictions to undertake similar initiatives. The lack of critical data on youth characteristics, including race and ethnicity, processing at various stages of the system, and outcomes, significantly impedes tracking and evaluation of reform activities. At the local level, a lack of transparency regarding the decisions of police, prosecutors, and judges makes it difficult to understand and improve system functioning. Advances in information technology allow organizations to share data, but the complex laws governing privacy and confidentiality, as well as entrenched organizational practices, create barriers to collaboration and efficiency.

The 2013 NRC report emphasized that support and leadership at the federal level are critically important to stimulate and sustain reforms within the juvenile justice system. Federal assistance is needed if state, tribal, and local jurisdictions are going to be able to put institutional structures in place and sustain effective practices aimed at keeping at-risk youths out of the juvenile justice system, providing developmentally appropriate environments for those that become involved in the system, and fostering collaborations among agencies that serve youths. The juvenile justice field needs enhanced technical assistance, training, and other kinds of consultative services to help achieve desired improvements. OJJDP has support from the field and the necessary congressional mandate to provide such assistance.

CHARGE TO THE COMMITTEE

At the request of the OJJDP administrator, the National Research Council (NRC) appointed an ad hoc committee to prepare a report that would distill the findings and conclusions in the 2013 NRC report and develop a strategic plan for its implementation by OJJDP, including a prioritized set of specific actions (see Appendix C for full list of committee members). Funding for the committee's study and report was provided by OJJDP, the Annie

E. Casey Foundation, and the John D. and Catherine T. MacArthur Foundation. The Committee on a Prioritized Plan to Implement a Developmental Approach in Juvenile Justice Reform was given the following task:

> An ad hoc committee will be convened to identify, assess and prioritize strategies and policies to effectively reform the juvenile justice system building on the recommendations from the 2013 report, *Reforming Juvenile Justice: A Developmental Approach*. The committee will assess the federal Office of Juvenile Justice and Delinquency Prevention's (OJJDP) activities and internal capacities to implement its legislative mandates on juvenile justice systems, policies, and practices; and, consult with experts and practitioners in the field of juvenile justice. The committee will also examine existing literature in three areas; implementation science, cross-agency collaboration and appropriate criteria for prioritization in the context of juvenile justice reform, including cost-benefit and cost-effectiveness analysis where applicable. The study will conclude with a report documenting the committee's findings and proposing recommendations for OJJDP and, where appropriate other federal agencies, to implement a reform plan using a developmental approach. The committee may address budgetary considerations and recommendations from other OJJDP plans.

The committee was specifically tasked with building on the research and recommendations of the 2013 NRC report and proposing a plan for OJJDP to implement reforms using a developmental approach. Taking a "developmental approach" to juvenile justice means effectuating the goals of the juvenile justice system (holding youths accountable, being fair, and preventing re-offending) in a way that is informed by, and compatible with, evolving knowledge about adolescent development and the research evidence on the effects of juvenile justice interventions. The 2013 NRC report consolidates scientific knowledge about adolescent development and systematically connects that body of research to the goals, policies, and practices of the juvenile justice system. This committee is relying upon the scientific findings, conclusions, and recommendations set forth in the 2013 report. Chapter 2 of this report briefly summarizes the 2013 report, distills the science behind what we are calling the "hallmarks" of a developmental approach, and sets forth a foundation for use by OJJDP and by states and localities to guide system reform.[3]

The statement of task also directed the committee to "assess [OJJDP's] activities and internal capacities to implement its legislative mandate on juvenile justice systems, policies and practices." The ability of the agency to fulfill its mandate is impacted by a number of external conditions, such as congressional directives to carry out other responsibilities aside from juvenile justice system improvement and the priorities and perspectives of the Department of Justice in successive administrations. It became evident early in the committee's deliberations that OJJDP does not currently have the capacity to lead and support nationwide juvenile justice reform if substantial portions of its limited funds and operations (under current appropriations and probably under any foreseeable appropriations) are devoted to tasks tangentially related to its legislative mandate relating to juvenile justice improvement and delinquency prevention. Trends in OJJDP's appropriated budget are discussed in Chapter 3. The committee decided, based on the JJDPA itself and the 2013 NRC report, that carrying out juvenile justice system improvement successfully could and should be OJJDP's top priority and that the committee's recommendations regarding the agency's priorities, budget, and operations would be formulated accordingly. OJJDP may be the most suitable agency in the Justice Department to carry out other congressionally mandated functions. However, the committee believes that these additional responsibilities should not be assigned in a way that compromises the agency's capacity to support and facilitate juvenile justice system improvement.

A question also arose regarding the extent to which the committee's strategic plan for implementing a developmentally informed approach to juvenile justice reform should encompass policies relating to the prosecution of juveniles in criminal court. "Juvenile justice reform" is generally understood to embrace a *developmentally informed approach to juvenile court jurisdictional issues, including transfer and sentencing of juveniles in criminal court*, an understanding reinforced by the Supreme Court's recent decisions in this area (*Roper v. Simmons*, 2005; *Graham v. Florida*, 2010; and *Miller v. Alabama*, 2012). The committee responsible for the 2013 NRC report chose to focus mainly on the design and operation of the juvenile justice system while offering general observa-

---

[3]See also Appendix B for a report brief describing the 2013 report and its findings and recommendations on research supporting, and the principles of, a developmental approach.

tions about the implications of a developmental approach for trial and punishment of juveniles in the criminal justice system. Specifically, the 2013 NRC report endorses a general presumption favoring original juvenile court jurisdiction in most cases involving offenders younger than 18 and a preference for individualized judicial decisions to transfer jurisdiction to a criminal court. This committee assumes that OJJDP will continue to interpret its mission to encompass activities designed to ameliorate policies and practices governing the decision to prosecute adolescents under the age of 18 in criminal courts.

Finally, the committee's charge included identifying strategies and policies that OJJDP might undertake to implement a reform plan using a developmental approach, in conjunction with other federal agencies both within and outside the Justice Department. The committee believes that a developmental approach is relevant to the treatment of adolescents over age 17 who are either within the dispositional and treatment jurisdiction of the juvenile court or who are prosecuted in a criminal court. From a developmental point of view, there is no single chronological age that marks the boundary between adolescence and adulthood. The processes of neurobiological and psychological maturation that are at the center of a developmental approach to young offenders occur well into their early twenties (Steinberg and Monahan, 2007; Steinberg and Scott, 2003).

TERMINOLOGY

As discussed further in Chapter 2, administration of juvenile justice is a complex system with multiple participants who are responsible for holding youths accountable for their offenses and administering to their needs. Each of these participants can bring a different perspective to what the system is and to their role in handling youths. In light of this complexity, the committee has defined certain terminology used in this report, much of which is commonly used in the juvenile justice field but often in different ways in different settings.

Juveniles

The 2013 NRC report (see pp. 18-19) laid out a number of definitions that this committee will continue to use. Thus, the committee uses the term "juvenile" synonymously with "young person" and "youth" to refer to anyone under the age of 18. Note, however, that "juvenile" typically also has a legal definition referring to individuals subject to the jurisdiction of juvenile or family court. The 2013 NRC report (p. 18) noted that ". . . adolescence has no finite chronological onset or end-point, and there is no legal definition of adolescence per se because the law regards different ages as being legally relevant in different contexts. The science of adolescence refers to a phase in development between childhood and adulthood beginning at puberty, typically about 12 or 13, and ending in the late teens or early 20s." Therefore, we use the term "adolescence" and "adolescent" to refer to teens or young adults. However, like the 2013 NRC report, the committee focuses on adolescents under age 18, given that 18 is the age of majority and the ceiling of delinquency adjudication in most states.

Delinquency Prevention

This report does not discuss the nature of offenses committed by youths or the sanctions given to them. However, the reader may find useful the definitions of delinquency and crime used in the 2013 NRC report (pp. 18-19):

> The term "delinquency" refers to acts by a juvenile that would be considered a crime if committed by an adult, as well as to actions that are illegal only because of the age of the offender. "Juvenile crime" or "criminal delinquency" refers to more serious acts that would be crimes if committed by adults. "Status delinquency" offenses include truancy, running away from home, incorrigibility (i.e., habitually disobeying reasonable and lawful commands of a parent, guardian, or custodian; also referred to in various statutes as unruly, uncontrollable, or ungovernable behavior), and liquor law violations.In some states, status delinquents are referred to the child welfare or social service systems, and in others status delinquents are dealt with in the juvenile justice system. "Adjudicated delinquent" or "delinquent" is used synonymously to describe the individual who has been found by the juvenile court to have committed a juvenile crime.

[The earlier report uses] the term "confinement," depending on the context, to refer to detention before adjudication or to placement in a custodial setting as a disposition after a finding of delinquency. In the dispositional context, it encompasses what are typically called institutional placements or out-of-home residential placements. It is not meant to encompass day treatment or nonresidential, community-based therapeutic programs.

Like the 2013 NRC report, this committee uses the term "justice-involved youths" to refer to youths who come into "contact" with any form of legal authority, including law enforcement, prosecutors, and intake personnel, even if no formal action is taken. We introduce the term "system-involved youths" for those youths who are referred to juvenile court or juvenile intake after police intake and a decision is made to file a formal petition and process the case within the juvenile justice system.

OJJDP has a mandate to undertake delinquency prevention; in defining delinquency prevention this committee found it useful to consider a standard typology of prevention used in public health (Institute of Medicine, 1994; National Research Council and Institute of Medicine, 2009). Preventive interventions are grouped in three broad categories: universal preventive interventions, selective preventive interventions, and indicated preventive interventions. "Universal interventions" are broad and target the general public or an entire population. "Selective interventions" target an individual or subgroup that exhibit significantly higher than average risk[4] prior to response or treatment. For purposes of this report, this would refer to times prior to any engagement in delinquent behavior or justice-system involvement, perhaps based on exposure to factors known to be risk factors for future delinquency. "Indicated interventions" target high-risk individuals and focus on the immediate risk and protective factors present in the individual's environment. The typology recognizes that preventive interventions are most effective when they are appropriately matched to their target population's level of risk—that is, when interventions focus upon reducing the risk factors and strengthening the protective factors that are most closely related to the problem being addressed (Institute of Medicine, 1994; National Research Council and Institute of Medicine, 2009).

The committee recognizes that OJJDP has a mandate under JJDPA to address delinquency prevention and to support programs that serve juveniles at risk of delinquency. In the past, the category of "at-risk" youths has sometimes been viewed broadly, encompassing what the public health model would characterize as "selective interventions" for youths viewed at elevated risk but not high risk of delinquency. The committee believes that the categories of youths targeted for delinquency prevention programs and services supported by OJJDP should be the youths *most at risk* of entering the juvenile justice system, such as (i) "justice-involved" youths at risk of formal system involvement and (ii) youths on an identifiable trajectory for system-involvement. In terms of the public health typology, the committee defines "delinquency prevention" under the JJDPA as encompassing "indicated interventions" for "high-risk" youths in these categories where the intervention is intended to prevent or reduce the risk of engaging in delinquency prior to the onset of formal justice system involvement. In addition, it bears emphasis that a core goal of juvenile justice is prevention of re-offending and, accordingly, a key role for OJJDP is to support "indicated interventions" aiming to prevent "system-involved youths" from further penetration in the system and to reduce repeat involvement in the system (recidivism). This was the role most emphasized in the 2013 NRC report.

System-Involved Families

This report focuses attention on family engagement. In so doing, we use the terms "system-involved families," "legacy families," and "families impacted by the system." The latter encompasses the former two. System-involved families are those immediate family members or adults in a guardian role for system-involved youths. System-involved families and youths have experiences and develop a certain kind of knowledge that cannot be appreciated by those who only work in or study the juvenile justice system. We use the term "legacy families" for families and youths that were once, but are no longer, system-involved and who possess this experiential knowledge, which can be useful for improving policies and practices. In addition to families, there are other participants who are not

---

[4]Risk has been defined as a characteristic at the biological, psychological, family, community, or cultural level that precedes and is associated with a higher likelihood of problem outcomes (Institute of Medicine, 1994; National Research Council and Institute of Medicine, 2009).

in the juvenile justice system per se but are influenced by or can influence the juvenile justice system and have a role in holding youths accountable and addressing their needs while the youths are system-involved and upon release from the system. These participants include school administrators and personnel, child welfare administrators and personnel, and community-based service providers. They are described in Chapter 2 and mentioned throughout the report.

STUDY METHODS

As set forth in its charge, this committee was formed for the specific purpose of "building on the recommendations from the 2013 report" in order to develop strategies for OJJDP to "implement a reform plan using a developmental approach." As a result, the committee drew upon the research and analysis of the 2013 NRC report, including the examination of OJJDP history and current capacity,[5] and augmented it with additional testimony and research.

The committee held four meetings during the course of the study. The first three were information-gathering meetings at which we heard presentations from a variety of stakeholders, including representatives from the Office of Justice Programs; OJJDP; the John D. and Catherine T. MacArthur Foundation; the Annie E. Casey Foundation; the Center for Children's Law and Policy; the National Conference of State Legislatures; the National Center for Juvenile Justice; the W. Haywood Burns Institute for Juvenile Justice, Fairness, and Equity; the Center for Juvenile Justice Reform; the Coalition for Juvenile Justice; and the Justice Policy Institute. See Appendix A for a full list of the speakers and interviews held by committee and staff. The fourth meeting was closed to the public so that the committee could deliberate on the report, finalize its conclusions and recommendations, and construct a prioritized plan with specific action steps as requested by the agency.

As part of its study, the committee engaged a consultant with more than 30 years of operational experience in the agency. It also commissioned a review and analysis of the federal budget to identify funding outside of OJJDP's budget that explicitly or implicitly targets at-risk and delinquent youths (Hayes, 2014; see discussion in Chapter 5). Although the 2013 NRC report served as primary background for the study (see Appendix B for the report brief and summary of key conclusions of the 2013 NRC report), the committee reviewed other relevant research literature on implementation science, interagency collaboration, change management, cost-benefit analysis, and budgetary prioritization. As noted in the 2013 NRC report, while the experiential evidence is impressive among jurisdictions that have made progress in reforming their systems, there is little systematic empirical evidence regarding the costs and outcomes of these reforms. Nonetheless, the committee notes that there is a research base that can guide juvenile justice reform (see Chapter 2):

> However, even in the absence of definitive evaluations of major reforms, the committee is convinced that the impressive body of research on adolescent development and the effects of juvenile justice interventions and programs is now sufficiently robust to provide a solid foundation for juvenile justice policy and for guiding policies and practices as knowledge continues to develop.
>
> (National Research Council, 2013, p. 321)

ORGANIZATION OF THE REPORT

The committee's report and guidance for OJJDP has been organized into five chapters. Following this introduction, Chapter 2 builds on the foundation of the 2013 NRC report and outlines the hallmarks of a developmental approach to juvenile justice. This chapter also summarizes OJJDP's role as a change agent for juvenile justice reform, to set the context for discussion in subsequent chapters. Chapter 3 focuses on the key improvements to OJJDP's operations, including budgetary considerations, needed to enable the agency to encourage and support juvenile justice reform. It examines how the philosophy of developmental science can guide all policies, practices,

---

[5]The 2013 NRC report analyzed both OJJDP's current status, particularly appropriations, carve-outs, earmarks, grant programs, granting capacity, research and data collection (National Research Council, 2013, pp. 308-320), and the conditions contributing to the agency's diminished capacity (pp. 281-308).

and decisions within the agency, as well as its research and technical assistance agendas. Chapter 4 considers ways that OJJDP can facilitate system change in individual jurisdictions through state leadership, which includes working with the state advisory groups, providing training and technical assistance, strengthening its approach to reducing racial and ethnic disparities, and supporting demonstration programs. Chapter 5 identifies agencies and organizations whose missions align with juvenile justice reform and highlights opportunities for OJJDP to reshape current collaborations and to establish important new partnerships. As requested by the agency, Chapter 6 provides a roadmap for OJJDP by assembling the report's recommendations specific to OJJDP and distilling action items from the chapters to provide a 3-year implementation plan.

2

Foundation for Change

BACKGROUND

Over the last few decades, there has been an explosion of empirical research on child and adolescent development in general and on the psychological and neurobiological basis of adolescent behavior in particular. In addition, a strong body of research has emerged on pathways of youths offending, the effectiveness of prevention and treatment programs, and the consequences of juvenile court interventions and of transfer of youths to criminal court for adult prosecution and sentencing. Taken as a whole, these findings raised many concerns over the extent to which the corrections-oriented philosophy of the 1980s and 1990s was an effective response to juvenile delinquency. By the start of the 21st century, as noted in Chapter 1, many localities and states had begun reforming their systems based on this impressive body of research on adolescent development and the effects of justice system interventions.

The National Research Council (NRC) Committee on Assessing Juvenile Justice Reform recognized in its 2013 report that adolescents differ from adults in three important ways. As compared with adults, adolescents are (1) less able to regulate their own behavior in emotionally charged contexts, (2) more sensitive to external influences to their own behavior such as the presence of peers and the immediacy of rewards, and (3) less able to make informed decisions that require long-term consideration (National Research Council, 2013, p. 2; hereafter, the 2013 NRC report). In general, these capacities improve as adolescents get older and progress into young adulthood.

That committee postulated that the overarching aim of the juvenile justice system is to support prosocial development of youths who come in contact with legal authorities or are involved in the system and thereby ensure the safety of communities. The specific goals of the juvenile court and affiliated agencies of the juvenile justice system are to hold youths accountable for wrongdoing, prevent further offending, and treat juveniles fairly (see National Research Council, 2013, pp. 4-7.) The 2013 NRC report demonstrated that all three goals of the juvenile justice system can be aligned with the emerging science of adolescent development. Specifically, the authors observed:

- Being held accountable for wrongdoing and accepting responsibility in a process perceived to be fair promotes healthy moral development and legal socialization.
- Being penalized, especially with severe sanctions, in a process perceived as unfair reinforces social disaffection and antisocial behavior.
- Predominantly punitive policies and programs do not foster prosocial development or reduce recidivism.

- No convincing evidence exists that confinement of juvenile offenders beyond the time needed to deliver intensive services reduces the likelihood of re-offending.
- Programs that aim to reduce risk factors associated with delinquency and violence, by fostering prosocial development and by building promotive (protective) factors at the individual, family, school, and peer levels, have been shown to be successful at preventing re-offending with benefits several times the costs.
- Racial and ethnic disparities, even if unintentional, contribute to perceptions of unfairness among justice-involved youth, their families, and members of minority communities.

(National Research Council, 2013, pp. 1-14)[1]

The 2013 NRC report further translated these findings into a set of guiding principles to offer actions that can be taken to achieve the goals of the juvenile justice system in a developmentally informed manner (see Box 11-1 in the 2013 report or the guiding principles box in Appendix B.) This process of applying what is known from developmental research on adolescence to policies and practices of juvenile justice is characterized, quite simply, as the developmental approach.

Although there have been policies and practices across the history of the juvenile justice system that were appropriate to the developmental needs of adolescents, this current period of reform is uniquely characterized as taking a developmental approach because of the growth in research knowledge on adolescent development and effective interventions as well as the rethinking of punitive policies from the 1980s and 1990s that have been shown to have adverse consequences on youth development and their re-offending (for further discussion on historical developments, see National Research Council, 2013, pp. 45-47).

The 2013 NRC report made four broad recommendations based on these findings and conclusions and on the central idea that a developmental approach should guide juvenile justice system improvement: (1) state and tribal governments should create oversight bodies to design, implement, and oversee a long-term process of juvenile justice reform; (2) the Office of Juvenile Justice and Delinquency Prevention (OJJDP) should assume a strengthened federal role to support juvenile justice system improvement; (3) federal agencies should support research to advance the science of adolescent development and improve understanding of effective responses to delinquency; and (4) OJJDP should guide a data improvement program. The report emphasized that laws, policies, and practices at every stage within the justice system should align with the evolving knowledge of adolescent development (National Research Council, 2013, Chapter 11).

This report focuses on OJJDP's role in implementing these recommendations, most notably how OJJDP can assume a strong leadership role and guide jurisdictions in the process of reform. In this chapter, the committee outlines a foundation for carrying out this facilitative role that draws on the literature of organizational and policy change as well as the principles for a developmentally informed juvenile justice system articulated in the 2013 NRC report.

HALLMARKS OF THE DEVELOPMENTAL APPROACH

Like the earlier 2013 NRC report and many advocates for reform, this committee envisions a juvenile justice system, guided by OJJDP, in which all participants understand the developmental differences between adolescents and adults and use that knowledge to create and use alternatives to juvenile system involvement, to provide the right services at the right time in the right setting for each youth who is formally involved in the system, and to ensure that every youth becomes a successful, productive member of the community. The committee that wrote the 2013 NRC report sought to articulate how the science of adolescent development can align with the goals of the juvenile justice system and produced a set of guiding principles for that purpose (see Box 11-1 in the 2013 report or the guiding principles box in Appendix B.)

This committee aims to show how the developmental approach can guide juvenile justice reform. To that end, we identified seven hallmarks of a developmental approach: (1) accountability without criminalization, (2) alternatives

---

[1]For more information, see the briefing slides of the 2013 NRC report. Available: http://sites.nationalacademies.org/DBASSE/CLAJ/dbasse_088932 [August 2014].

to justice system involvement, (3) individualized response based on assessment of needs and risks, (4) confinement only when necessary for public safety, (5) a genuine commitment to fairness, (6) sensitivity to disparate treatment, and (7) family engagement. While these hallmarks draw from and complement the guiding principles from the 2013 NRC report, we found it useful to have a distinct list of hallmarks that captures what is currently known from developmental science and that can be pulled out easily for policy and programmatic discussions. The rationale and intended meaning of each hallmark are explained below.

Accountability Without Criminalization

Holding offenders accountable is predicated on the universally recognized precept that persons who cause harm, especially serious personal victimization, should be held responsible and accountable and that their behavior should be subject to corrective action. Although confinement is one option for holding adolescents accountable for their actions, it should be used sparingly and only when public safety concerns are especially heightened (see discussion below). The 2013 NRC report documents that, in order to develop into prosocial adults who appreciate the legitimacy of justice systems, adolescents need opportunities to accept responsibility for their actions and, where appropriate, to make amends to affected individuals and communities. Having a criminal record impedes education and employment opportunities, disrupts relationships, and limits access to social services (National Research Council, 2013, 2014). Given that adolescence is a transient period, official records of a juvenile's encounters with the juvenile justice system should be strictly confidential, except in extraordinary circumstances involving a compelling need to protect public safety, so as to fully preserve the youth's opportunities for successful integration into adult life.

Alternatives to Justice System Involvement

Knowledge is growing about the effectiveness of interventions designed to improve decision making and those designed to address health and mental health problems of youths (National Research Council, 2013; National Research Council and Institute of Medicine, 2009). Interventions aiming to prevent re-offending often are more effective if services needed by adolescents are provided with minimal penetration into the system, as long as accountability is also achieved when appropriate. The 2013 NRC report notes that well-designed community-based programs are more likely than institutional confinement to facilitate healthy development and reduce recidivism for the majority of youths who come to the attention of the juvenile justice system (National Research Council, 2013, Chapter 6). It is important to recognize that programs or facilities in which justice-involved youths are placed provide the "social context" for their ongoing development and that interventions should be designed to provide positive influences and to strengthen available family relationships and supports.

Responses by law enforcement and school disciplinary personnel should be governed by the "first, do no harm" axiom that is inherent in a developmental approach; an approach consistent with this is to routinely and informally divert youths suspected of less serious offending to parental supervision or other community resources in lieu of initiating the juvenile justice process. Pre-petition diversion is an effective and often used approach for nonviolent, first time offenders (National Research Council, 2013). However there is also potential to develop procedures for post-petition diversion which, if coupled with an automatic expungement upon successful completion of the diversion program, would achieve accountability without criminalization.[2]

Individualized Response Based on Assessment of Needs and Risks

Once youths become involved in the juvenile justice system, a range of decision makers play a role in the response (see Box 2-1). Individualized assessment of the treatment and intervention needs of the adolescent, as well as the risk of subsequent offending, helps to match needs (particularly those associated with the likelihood

---

[2]See DC CODE § 16-2305.01(3), which provides for diversion as a noncriminal alternative to adjudication. Available: http://dccode.org/simple/sections/16-2305.html [July 2014].

BOX 2-1
Participants in the Juvenile Justice Process

The juvenile process involves a range of decision makers and participants who interact with adolescents who are at various stages of cognitive and emotional development. Training justice personnel and associated service providers on findings from developmental science can help them understand adolescent behavior and how best to respond to youths involved in the system. Instituting policies informed by developmental science can lead to practices that hold adolescents accountable for their actions and administer services consistent with needs while promoting prosocial development.

- **Community-based service providers** (e.g., mental health and drug treatment providers, educators, and employment services providers) offer and administer treatment to juveniles placed outside the home, sometimes as options for diversion out of juvenile justice, as well as after youths become system involved. Assignments to programming should be based on a careful assessment of each adolescent's needs for a successful transition back into the family and community.
- **Defense counsel** stand in a unique position in that they can gather a lot of the requisite information regarding the youth's background and life circumstances, including the nature of the criminal event and the circumstances surrounding the adolescent's motivation. Defense counsel also can help to explain the juvenile court proceedings to adolescents and their families. They prepare material for the court regarding the youth's competency to rationally understand and engage in the proceedings against him/her and mount the appropriate defense.
- **Judges** play a central role in any case in which a delinquency petition is filed. Depending upon the jurisdiction, judges have substantial power to determine whether diversion is an option. If the case continues to court, judges have responsibility to ensure that the court process is fair, that individualized determinations are made, and that adolescents and their families understand all aspects of the court proceeding and their options and are given a voice in the process.
- **Juvenile justice case managers** supervise system-involved youths who are living in their homes or communities and coordinate the provision of community-based services such as tutoring, vocational services, family counseling, mentoring, and mental health or behavioral health services. Assessments and assignments should be based on a careful understanding of each adolescent's needs for a successful transition back into the family and community.
- **Law enforcement officers** have a unique opportunity to practice procedural justice so that interactions are fair and just and follow the law and legal procedure. They can also make individual judgments whether to divert youths to services agencies or parental control without initiating formal system involvement.
- **Prosecutors** wield a sizable amount of power and discretion in that they can divert or charge adolescents with various crime types and also, where it is an option, can transfer the adolescent to adult criminal court for processing. Prosecutors using a developmental approach will make individualized determinations that balance holding youths accountable for their actions with providing the interventions they may need, while taking into account the developmental differences between adolescents and adults.
- **Residential facilities** provide out-of-home placement for system-involved youths. Depending on the state, out-of-home placement can refer to shelter programs (typically 24 hours to 30 days), residential treatment programs (e.g., mental health or behavioral health treatment, substance abuse treatment), correctional facilities (detention or pre-adjudication and commitment or post-disposition), foster homes (family-based), or group homes. Residential facilities provide a more developmentally appropriate environment by ensuring that all placement staff are trained to understand normal adolescent risk-taking behavior and the developmental need for prosocial interactions between peers and with adults and opportunities for decision making.
- **School administrators and personnel**, including teachers, guidance counselors, coaches, administrators, and school-based officers, are involved on the front end and also on the back end when youths are returned to their communities and schools. With appropriate training, they are positioned to know when to engage the juvenile justice system versus other services based on assessment of risk and needs of the youths.

of further offending) appropriately to available levels of supervision and services (Aos et al., 2004; Howell, 2009; Mulvey, 2005; Mulvey and Iselin, 2008; Office of Juvenile Justice and Delinquency Prevention, 1995). Collection of a wide variety of information ensures a more dynamic view of adolescents and their behaviors and reflects a shift from predicting risk (20th-century juvenile justice) to managing risk (21st-century developmentally informed juvenile justice). This approach places less emphasis on categories of offending and more emphasis on the malleable factors that may contribute to antisocial behavior in each case.

These assessments also can identify factors that help to differentiate youths at lower risk of re-offending—who can be handled through diversion or in community-based settings from higher-risk youths—for whom more intensive and/or expansive interventions should be provided. The use of these tools focuses system resources where they are most likely to provide a return in reduced offending and positive adolescent development. Successful matching of the adolescent to requisite services (e.g., with validated risk/need assessment tools) is thus critical for several goals: successful treatment, reintegration into the community, and reduced recidivism.

Among youths charged with serious offenses who are subject to prosecution in the criminal justice system, individualized determinations by prosecutors and judges are needed about whether an adolescent will be tried as an adult and what sentence is imposed upon conviction in a criminal court. These judgments would take into account the features of adolescent decision making and judgment that affect their culpability and amenability to change, compared with adults who have committed similar transgressions (Grisso et al., 2003; National Research Council, 2013, pp. 130-136; Scott and Grisso, 2005).[3]

Confinement Only When Necessary for Public Safety

Consistent research findings show that negative effects and outcomes for juveniles are associated with lengthy confinement and severe conditions. In extreme cases, youths who are confined have been exposed to sexual abuse, extended isolation or solitary confinement, use of restraints, inadequate educational and behavioral health services, and untrained staff (American Civil Liberties Union, 2013; Beck et al., 2013; National Evaluation and Technical Assistance Center, 2010; Wasserman et al., 2004). According to the 2013 NRC report (National Research Council, 2013, p. 155):

> . . . institutional treatment programs generally have an unimpressive record for reducing reoffending and that large, overcrowded facilities with limited treatment programs (in which custody trumps treatment concerns) often have high recidivism rates (Ezell, 2007; Trulson et al., 2007). At the same time, there are empirically sound and convincing reports indicating that theoretically grounded, adequately staffed, and well-documented programs for seriously violent youth that involve institutional care can produce impressive and fiscally advantageous effects (Barnoski, 2004; Caldwell, Vitaceo, and Van Rybrock, 2006; Caldwell et al., 2006).

As noted above, a key hallmark of a developmental approach to juvenile justice reform is developing alternatives to justice system involvement. Even when youths are adjudicated as delinquent, alternatives to confinement often serve the goals of the system. This does not necessitate all service provision being outside of placement settings, as residential placement of some adolescents is necessary from a public safety perspective. Studies have shown, however, that confinement of juveniles beyond the minimum amount needed to deliver intensive services effectively is not only wasteful economically but also potentially harmful, and it may impede prosocial development (National Research Council, 2013). When adolescents are assigned to residential placements, their environments should be conducive to positive development as well as providing appropriate services and treatment to address

---

[3]The Supreme Court's recent decisions in *Roper v. Simmons* (2005), *Graham v. Florida* (2010), and *Miller v. Alabama* (2012) emphasize that adolescents' diminished culpability and amenability to change preclude the most severe punishments altogether and also should discourage lengthy mandatory sentences. As noted by the 2013 NRC report, this principle also should require individualized assessment of a juvenile as a prerequisite to trial in criminal court. See, for example, *Roper v. Simmons* (2005), p. 568, where the Supreme Court recognized that the choices of adolescents are influenced by factors integral to their stage of development, stating ". . . blameworthiness is diminished, to a substantial degree, by reason of youth and immaturity," and *Graham v. Florida* (2010), pp. 50-51, where the Supreme Court recognized that a juvenile offender may exhibit a "capacity for change" and should be given "a chance to demonstrate maturity and reform."

their needs. One way to ensure such environments is through standards for facilities. Performance-based standards, as discussed in the 2013 NRC report, provide an example of a juvenile corrections data collection system that has been highly effective. These standards include standard measures in areas such as education, safety, behavior management, service provision, and resource connections, and they use analytical tools that allow comparisons of facilities within a state and across states.

A Genuine Commitment to Fairness

Ensuring fairness is important in individual cases and also throughout the administration of justice more generally. Empirical studies have found that treating youths fairly and ensuring that they perceive that they have been treated fairly and with dignity contribute to several important features of prosocial development, including moral development, belief in the legitimacy of the law, and the legal socialization process more generally (National Research Council, 2013, pp. 183-210). A developmentally informed juvenile justice system and its personnel would ensure that adolescents are represented by properly trained counsel, understand the proceedings in their entirety, appreciate their own jeopardy, and are able to participate meaningfully in their own cases throughout the process (Grisso et al., 2003; Scott and Grisso, 2005). Fairness could also be ensured by formulating and implementing performance measures throughout the process to ascertain whether victims, justice-involved youths, and their families perceive that they were treated fairly and to assess perceptions and attitudes of relevant communities regarding the fairness, as well as effectiveness, of the juvenile justice system.

Sensitivity to Disparate Treatment

In ensuring fairness, jurisdictions' efforts to reduce racial and ethnic disparities are extremely important because perceptions of unfairness are so deep and so corrosive to minorities, their families, and communities. As discussed in Chapters 3 and 4, the federal government and many jurisdictions are interested in reducing racial and ethnic disparities in juvenile justice system involvement. Efforts to reduce disparities have included monitoring of rates of system involvement and confinement overall and among minorities and implementing policy changes to reduce unnecessary system involvement or confinement, particularly where such responses have had an uneven impact on minorities. Although actions by the juvenile justice system, as acknowledged in the 2013 NRC report, are only part of a much larger array of forces that lead to these disparities, a developmentally informed system can ameliorate the effects of disadvantage and discrimination by reducing unnecessary system involvement and confinement (National Research Council, 2013, p. 239):

> The literature reflects continuing uncertainty about the relative contribution of differential offending, differential enforcement and processing, and structural inequalities to these disparities. However, the current body of research suggests that poverty, social disadvantage, neighborhood disorganization, constricted opportunities, and other structural inequalities—which are strongly correlated with race/ethnicity—contribute to both differential offending and differential selection, especially at the front end of juvenile justice decision making. Because bias (whether conscious or unconscious) also plays a role, albeit of unknown magnitude, juvenile justice officials should embrace activities designed to increase awareness of these unconscious biases and to counteract them, as well as to detect and respond effectively to overt instances of discrimination. Although the juvenile justice system itself cannot alter the underlying structural causes of racial/ethnic disparities in juvenile justice, many conventional practices in enforcement and administration magnify these underlying disparities, and these contributors *are* within the reach of justice system policy makers.

Family Engagement

During adolescence, family and peer influences as well as school and community influences operate in interconnected and complex ways in youth development. "Family can provide a source of supervision, guidance, and protection" (National Research Council, 2013, p. 117). A positive family experience is a central feature of positive youth development, even for system-involved youths. A number of community-based treatment programs with positive effects on reducing recidivism include the youth's family in the program and give attention to features of the youth's social environment (National Research Council, 2013). Evidence from the mental health and child welfare fields indicates that familial involvement throughout system processes can lead to better outcomes for youths (Burns et al., 1995; Dawson and Berry, 2002; Kemp et al., 2009; Robertson, 2005). The juvenile justice system has the opportunity and responsibility to encourage family involvement whenever possible, including interactions with law enforcement, court proceedings, service delivery, intervention, and re-integration, in order to produce successful outcomes and reduced re-offending. Parent(s) and/or other family members should be involved in individual cases (to the extent deemed necessary and legally appropriate) and should have an opportunity to participate throughout the process of delivering services to the youth and the family. According to the 2013 NRC report (National Research Council, 2013, p. 159):

> [g]iven all that is known regarding the significance of parenting and of the parent-child relationship, expecting that a youth [within the juvenile justice system] might experience significant and lasting change with only superficial family involvement seems illogical. The juvenile justice system, however, appears to have a long way to go toward integrating parents and families into interventions and court processes. Despite the centrality of parental involvement in many successful programs, focus groups reveal that parents continue to be, or perceive being, blamed for the youth's problems, to be regarded as obstacles, and to be insufficiently involved in crucial decision-making and planning processes during disposition, placement, and preparation for aftercare.

Some efforts to involve families in system processes are under way, but models for family engagement are in the early stages of development. Not all families are similarly situated and have the requisite resources or equal desire for involvement. However, a developmentally informed system and its personnel would aggressively seek to work with all families and family-focused organizations based on the understanding that they are necessary and critical partners. As a whole, these hallmark features of a developmental approach to juvenile justice provide a vision to guide system reform.

THE MISSION OF OJJDP

OJJDP had been the driver of juvenile justice improvement in the 20th century. Since then, reform has been propelled forward by a combination of drivers, including vanguard initiatives in several states and localities, civil rights litigation, and most importantly, transformative investments by foundations (National Research Council, 2013, Chapters 9 and 10). However, major investments made by philanthropic organizations are likely to diminish significantly in the coming years. In the committee's view, the time is right for OJJDP to take the lead in a nationwide effort to facilitate, support, and sustain developmentally oriented juvenile justice reform. OJJDP should begin to develop and enhance the capabilities that will be needed to carry out the activities that have characterized the foundations' commitments: supporting program innovation and policy development, disseminating knowledge, providing technical assistance for reform, convening stakeholders, and facilitating consensus building.

This report addresses two types of institutional change. The first, and primary focus of this report, is the change needed within the federal government and particularly within OJJDP to enable the agency to facilitate juvenile justice reform in states and other jurisdictions. The second is the change that will be needed to achieve reform at the state, local, and tribal levels and within individual agencies that are part of the complex relationships that comprise local juvenile justice systems. Both types of change have to be undertaken in a concerted and planned way, informed by what is known about effective juvenile justice and intervention practices and about facilitating and implementing institutional change in general. Ingrained structures, cultures, and routines can present significant obstacles and resistance to change (Marquis and Tilcsik, 2013). Unsupportive policies, regulations, or funding directives from entities external to but with authority for an institution (e.g., the Department of Justice for OJJDP or the governor's office for a state system) can also present obstacles to change (Fixsen et al., 2005; National Research Council and Institute of Medicine, 2009).

To be successful, institutional change and reform should be based on specific and concrete steps shown to be effective in large organizations. Knowledge about managing change and the science of implementation are far from complete: there are only a handful of case studies and summary reports and virtually none that describe and rigorously evaluate reform and systems change in a program agency such as OJJDP, which exists in a much larger agency, the Office of Justice Programs, of the U.S. Department of Justice. However, the research is sufficiently robust to offer general guidance on institutionalizing a new culture and a new way of operating to overcome the inevitable challenges.

Within the body of literature on changing organizations and systems, a number of models exist to describe the change process. More recent models argue that change should be seen as a process of learning instead of distinct stages (Barnard and Stoll, 2010). However, even these models offer a sequence of actions. In a comparison of models, Todnem (2005) observed that creating a vision and operationalizing that vision through policies and cultural structures were common across all models examined. While a clear vision can initiate institutional change, implementing and sustaining change will require resources aligned to the vision as well as stakeholder support (Todnem, 2005). Although these basic principles may seem obvious, studies have shown that they can be overlooked or their importance underestimated by leaders or managers looking to implement change (Fernandez and Rainey, 2006; Kotter 1995, 1996).

GUIDING REFORM IN STATES, LOCALITIES, AND TRIBES

Helping states, tribal jurisdictions, and localities implement and sustain developmentally oriented policies and programs is an important part of OJJDP's mandated role and should be encompassed by the services and guidance OJJDP provides. This is not an easy task, and in a system as complex as the juvenile justice system—with its myriad patterns and variations present in each of the 50 states, the District of Columbia, tribal jurisdictions, and territories and possessions, as well as variations at the local level—many challenges will present themselves along the way toward this goal.

As detailed in the 2013 NRC report (pp. 269-279), the organizational culture of juvenile justice agencies may impede innovations; many lack the leadership, staff capacity, or resources to enact and sustain meaningful reform over time. Policies and practices based on a confinement-oriented correctional approach may still exist in tandem with polices aimed at increasing the use of community-based services. This creates cultural tensions and obstacles that will need to be resolved to achieve reform. In addition, although many reforms promise budgetary savings, implementing change can often be an added cost in the short run. Structural barriers between participants in the juvenile justice system at different levels of government, as well as issues that arise from the separation of legislative and executive powers, may also present challenges for reforms. The differences between juvenile justice agencies; the courts; and other family, health, and welfare agencies make collaboration difficult and often require structural and bureaucratic changes and a recognition of shared goals and vision among partners before reform can take hold. Implementing a developmental approach presents unique challenges because certain justice system stakeholders will invariably be resistant to change. As the transformation from an institution-based correctional model to a community-based services model proceeds, experience from efforts to close state prisons and mental health facilities demonstrates that often local governments, correctional workers' unions, and legislators who support the unions may be opposed to the resulting shifts. Similarly, as community-based service models take hold, many jurisdictions have difficulty identifying programs at the local level capable of providing necessary services, including secure residential programs.

A historical review of the juvenile justice system shows that a number of drivers—although they surely are not the sole factors influencing change—have provided an impetus for reform throughout the years. In recent years, civil rights litigation, transformational state models, influential foundation initiatives, and community advocacy, in response to mounting scientific evidence, have pushed reform agendas in many state and local juvenile justice systems. There is no magic formula for success, of course, and different approaches may be fruitful. However, the 2013 NRC report observed that one promising formula for achieving system change would include the following elements: cultivating strong and influential leadership; building consensus among stakeholders; nurturing grassroots support; shaping and being responsive to public opinion on key reform issues; and incorporating data-driven policies, models, and evaluations (for more discussion, see National Research Council, 2013, pp. 244-266).

Clarity of vision and consensus on the goals of that vision are integral prerequisites to change. Without consensus and buy-in from stakeholders at all levels, reform efforts will be at cross-purposes and can be easily undermined and discarded. A range of different stakeholders work within juvenile justice; their level of interest and capacity to support system change may vary. The use of data for description and information and the dissemination of research results in ways that may be consumed across a range of constituents are critical functions in the systems change process. OJJDP cannot direct change, but it can be in a position to guide jurisdictions to a state of readiness, help them build the necessary capacity and knowledge, and support state and local leaders when they are ready to implement reform.

CONCLUSION

In this report, the committee presents a roadmap for OJJDP to redefine itself as a "change agent" for juvenile justice reform. The roadmap has three parts, which will be presented in greater depth in Chapters 3, 4, and 5. Each part can be understood as answering a specific question: First, what should OJJDP do to prepare itself organizationally? Second, what should OJJDP do to facilitate and support system change in states, tribal jurisdictions, and localities? Third, what should OJJDP do to forge the collaborative partnerships with other federal agencies and stakeholder groups that will be needed to leverage its own resources, promote consensus-building, and harness the energies and activities of these organizations to facilitate a developmental approach to juvenile justice reform?

3

Refocusing the Office of Juvenile Justice and Delinquency Prevention

With authorization from the Juvenile Justice and Delinquency Prevention Act of 1974, as amended (JJDPA), the Office of Juvenile Justice and Delinquency Prevention (OJJDP) is the congressionally mandated lead agency for juvenile justice. The current statutory purpose is threefold: "(1) to support State and local programs that prevent juvenile involvement in delinquent behavior; (2) to assist State and local governments in promoting public safety by encouraging accountability for acts of juvenile delinquency; and (3) to assist State and local governments in addressing juvenile crime through the provision of technical assistance, research, training, evaluation, and the dissemination of information on effective programs for combating juvenile delinquency" (P.L. 93-415, 42 U.S.C. §5602). Under this authority, OJJDP has the multiple roles of administering programs; assisting states, localities, and tribal governments; and supporting research. It also has the dual purpose of addressing delinquency prevention as well as juvenile justice system improvements.

OJJDP states that it accomplishes its statutory mandate through the provision of ". . . national leadership, coordination and resources to prevent and respond to juvenile delinquency and victimization."[1] Ultimately, given the breadth of its purpose, the agency's ability to accomplish its tasks is largely tied to the resources and collaborative efforts that it can invest in the areas selected as priorities. The resources that are available to OJJDP are its staff and the funding and programs it makes available to grantees. OJJDP can also draw on partnerships with other federal agencies and national organizations (see discussion in Chapter 5).

The JJDPA lays out four core protections of youths with which states must comply to receive OJJDP's formula and categorical funds for improvements to their juvenile justice systems: deinstitutionalization of status offenders, removal of juveniles from adult jail and lockup, sight and sound separation from adult inmates in institutional settings, and the requirement for addressing disproportionate minority contact (see Box 3-1). As noted in the 2013 National Research Council (NRC) report, these protections reflect developmentally appropriate practices.

For over a decade, appropriations for the agency and its grant programs have declined. In addition, at the direction of Congress and the U.S. Department of Justice, OJJDP has taken on increased responsibilities. The combination of diminishing resources and growing responsibilities has reduced the agency's ability to support juvenile justice system improvement[2] (see further discussion later in this chapter).

---

[1]OJJDP's mission statement available: http://www.ojjdp.gov/about/missionstatement.html [April 2014].

[2]In response to a question about OJJDP's role in the reform efforts that have been occurring throughout the nation, a panel presenting to the committee unanimously stated that the agency has not played a significant role in the system improvements, which have occurred largely through the support and efforts of foundations. (Presentation to the committee by the Advocacy panelists on February 14, 2014. See Appendix A for a list of speakers and interviews.)

BOX 3-1
The JJDPA's Four Core Protections

- Deinstitutionalization of status offenders: Juveniles who are charged with or who have committed an offense that would not be a crime if committed by an adult and juveniles who are not charged with any offenses are not to be placed in secure detention or secure correctional facilities.
- Juveniles are not to be detained or confined in any institution in which they would have contact with adult inmates. Additionally, correctional staff working with both adult and juvenile offenders in collocated facilities must have been trained and certified to work with juveniles.
- Juveniles are not to be detained or confined in any jail or lockup for adults, except for temporary holds of juveniles who are accused of non–status offenses. These juveniles may be detained for no longer than 6 hours as they are processed, waiting to be released, awaiting transfer to a juvenile facility, or awaiting an initial court appearance. Additionally, juveniles in rural locations may be held for up to 48 hours in jails or lockups for adults as they await their initial court appearance. Juveniles held in adult jails or lockups in both rural and urban areas are not to have sight or sound contact with adult inmates, and any staff working with both adults and juveniles in collocated facilities must have been trained and certified to work with juveniles.
- Disproportionate minority contact: States are required to show that they are implementing juvenile delinquency prevention programs designed to reduce the disproportionate representation of minority youth who come into contact with the juvenile justice system at all levels of processing—without establishing or requiring numerical standards or quotas.

SOURCE: Nuñez-Neto (2008).

This chapter reviews OJJDP's statutory authority, capacity, and current operations and sets forth a blueprint for refocusing OJJDP's activities so that it can successfully guide juvenile justice reform based on a developmental approach (see discussion in Chapter 2). The chapter first addresses two ways in which congressional action could significantly enhance OJJDP's capacity to implement the strategic plan outlined in this report: first, by reauthorizing the agency and thereby reaffirming and strengthening its authority, and second, by approving a budget that gives the agency sufficient resources to carry out its mission, particularly the role envisioned here of facilitating juvenile justice reform and system improvements. The chapter then presents the key components of a strategic plan for OJJDP: enhancing staff capacity and refocusing each of the agency's programs and activities to adequately support juvenile justice system improvement. Such an agenda will require attention to the agency's training and technical assistance, grant making, demonstration grants, data collection and research programs, and information dissemination, each of which is reviewed below.

REAUTHORIZING AND STRENGTHENING OJJDP

The 2013 NRC report characterizes ". . . OJJDP as being in a state of decline both in capacity and stature . . . OJJDP's 2002 authorizing legislation (P.L. 107-273) expired in 2007 and 2008, although funding support has continued [under annual appropriation acts]. Numerous efforts to reauthorize the agency have been unsuccessful" (National Research Council, 2013, p. 314). Nonetheless, the juvenile justice field continues to support reauthorization and a renewed leadership role for OJJDP.

Although much of what is recommended in this report can be accomplished under the current statutory framework, reauthorization of the JJDPA would establish a firm foundation for OJJDP's role in the transformative work ahead, as well as signaling to the field that the nation has entered the next stage in juvenile justice reform based upon the research and science of adolescent development. The reauthorizing legislation should identify support for juvenile justice system improvements based on the science of adolescent development and on evidence regarding the effects of justice system interventions. Reauthorization of JJDPA with updated legislative language would send a strong message regarding the need for state, local, and tribal governments to assume greater responsibility for administering a developmentally appropriate juvenile justice system as a condition for federal support. The 2013 NRC report made two broad recommendations regarding the reauthorization of the JJDPA: restoring the authority of the office through reauthorization, appropriations, and funding flexibility, and strengthening the core protections (see Box 3-2). This committee underscores these previous recommendations with additional suggestions to clarify and strengthen the JJDPA. The suggestions are based on findings from the earlier 2013 NRC report, as well as findings presented in this report as noted. A reauthorized JJDPA should

- Require the OJJDP administrator to develop objectives, priorities, and a long-term plan to improve the juvenile justice system in the United States, taking account of scientific knowledge regarding adolescent development and behavior and regarding the effects of delinquency prevention programs and juvenile justice interventions on adolescent behavior and well-being. (See Chapter 2.)
- Require state plans to describe how the plan is supported by, or takes account of, scientific knowledge regarding adolescent development and behavior and regarding the effects of delinquency prevention programs and juvenile justice interventions on adolescent behavior and well-being. (See Chapter 4 on nurturing state leadership.)
- Require State Advisory Groups to include members who have training, experience, or special knowledge concerning adolescent development. (See Chapter 4 on nurturing state leadership.)
- Require State Advisory Groups to have at least two members of families of youths who have been involved in the juvenile justice system and at least two youths who have been involved in the juvenile justice system. (See Chapter 4 on nurturing state leadership and Chapter 5 on family engagement.[3])
- Exclude from the definition of "adult inmate" an individual who, at the time of the offense, was younger than the maximum age at which a youth can be held in a juvenile facility under applicable state law and who was committed to the care and custody of a juvenile correctional agency by a court of competent jurisdiction or by operation of applicable state law. (See National Research Council, 2013, pp. 296-297.)
- Modify the "status offense" provision to preclude placement in secure detention facilities or secure correctional facilities of juveniles who have been charged with or committed offenses that would not be punishable if committed by a person of age 21 or older or that would not be punishable by confinement if committed by an adult. (See National Research Council, 2013, pp. 294-296.)
- Modify the "status offense" provision to eliminate the exception for juveniles who have violated a "valid court order" or have been charged with doing so. (See National Research Council, 2013, pp. 294-296.)

When OJJDP is reauthorized, it should be directed, as recommended by the 2013 NRC report, to base its programs and activities on the scientific knowledge regarding adolescent development and the effects of delinquency prevention programs and juvenile justice interventions; to link state plans and training of State Advisory Groups to the accumulating knowledge about adolescent development; to modify the definitions for "status offenses" and for an "adult inmate" so that all adolescents are treated appropriately; and to identify support for developmentally informed juvenile justice system improvement as one of the agency's responsibilities.

TRENDS IN OJJDP'S FUNDING

The history of OJJDP's total funding is shown in Figure 3-1. Since its creation, OJJDP has provided funding through formula grants to participating states and territories to help them meet the goals of the JJDPA and improve

---

[3]Note that the "at least two members of families" requirement is designed to provide for the perspective of legacy families on the SAGs while addressing concerns raised to the committee that a single representative may be perceived as "tokenism" and places too great a burden on one person to represent all families. With two representatives, the commitment to families is underscored and allows for peers to share the responsibility. (Presentation to committee by Family stakeholders on February 13, 2014.)

BOX 3-2
2013 NRC Report Recommendations for the
Reauthorization of the Juvenile Justice and Delinquency Prevention Act

Recommendation 2: The role of OJJDP in preventing delinquency and supporting juvenile justice improvement should be strengthened.

a. OJJDP's capacity to carry out its core mission should be restored through reauthorization, appropriations, and funding flexibility. Assisting state, local, and tribal jurisdictions to align their juvenile justice systems with evolving knowledge about adolescent development and implementing evidence-based and developmentally informed policies, programs, and practices should be among the agency's top priorities. Any additional responsibilities and authority conferred on the agency should be amply funded so as not to erode the funds needed to carry out the core mission.

b. OJJDP's legislative mandate to provide core protections should be strengthened through reauthorizing legislation that defines status offenses to include offenses such as possession of alcohol or tobacco that apply only to youths under 21; precludes without exception the detention of youths who commit offenses that would not be punishable by confinement if committed by an adult; modifies the definition of an adult inmate to give states flexibility to keep youths in juvenile facilities until they reach the age of extended juvenile court jurisdiction; and expands the protections to all youths under age 18 in pretrial detention, whether charged in juvenile or in adult courts.

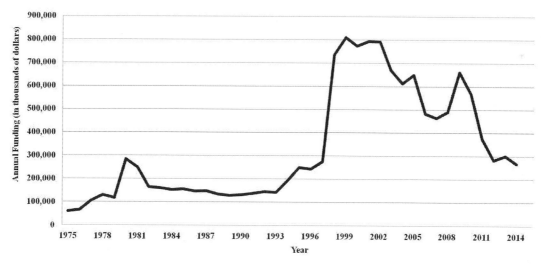

FIGURE 3-1 Office of Juvenile Justice and Delinquency Prevention appropriations in 2014 constant dollars.
SOURCE: Adapted from National Research Council (2013, Figure 10-1, pp. 287) and updated with recent funding totals from the Office of Juvenile Justice and Delinquency Prevention.

their juvenile justice systems. These funds, authorized under Title II, Part B, of the JJDPA, can be applied to a wide variety of activities for both delinquency prevention and interventions for youths who come into contact with legal authorities and the system (i.e., justice-involved youths), including but not limited to activities to comply with the core protections (Office of Juvenile Justice and Delinquency Prevention, 2014).

Today, OJJDP receives appropriations for a number of programs in addition to its Formula Grants Program for states (see Table 3-1). Within each of these major grant programs, the funding is further subdivided into multiple grant awards and efforts supporting many different program priorities and needs across the country that may (1) address risk factors associated with delinquency; (2) protect missing, exploited, or abused children; (3) prevent and control delinquency; or (4) improve practices and outcomes for system-involved juveniles. A few of the programs are designed specifically to provide training and technical assistance (e.g., those authorized through the Missing Children's Assistance Act and Victims of Child Abuse Act). The Juvenile Accountability Block Grant (JABG) Program, authorized in 1992, provided funding to OJJDP that could be administered to the states to implement systems of graduated sanctions and other accountability-based programs. "For five years, monies appropriated through JABG represented a significant boost to OJJDP's budget and, very important, [were] a source of funding states relied on to build and strengthen their juvenile justice system infrastructure" (National Research Council, 2013, p. 286).

TABLE 3-1 OJJDP Funding by Fiscal Year (FY) (thousands of dollars [actual])

OJJDP Appropriations	FY 2011	FY 2012	FY 2013	FY 2014
Juvenile Justice Programs				
Part B-Formula Grants & State TA	62,126	40,000	44,000	55,500
[Emergency Planning Detention Facilities]	—	—	[500]	[500]
Youth Mentoring	82,834	78,000	90,000	88,500
Title V-Local Delinquency Prevention	53,842	20,000	20,000	15,000
Incentive Grants	[4,141]	[0]	[0]	[0]
Tribal Youth Program	[20,709]	[10,000]	[10,000]	[5,000]
Alcohol Prevention/EUDL[a]	[20,709]	[5,000]	[5,000]	[2,500]
Gang Prevention/OJJDP	[8,283]	[5,000]	[5,000]	[2,500]
Juvenile Justice Education Collaboration	[0]	[0]	[0]	[5,000]
Juvenile Accountability Block Grant	45,559	30,000	25,000	[0]
Missing and Exploited Children	69,860	65,000	67,000	67,000
Safe Start	4,141	0	0	0
Child Abuse Training for Judicial Personnel	—	1,500	1,500	1,500
Improving Investigation & Prosecution of Child Abuse	18,638	18,000	19,000	19,000
National Forum on Youth Violence Prevention	—	2,000	2,000	1,000
Children of Incarcerated Parents Web Portal	—	—	—	500
Girls in the Justice System	—	—	—	1,000
Community-Based Violence Prevention	8,283	8,000	11,000	5,500
Subtotal	345,283	262,500	279,500	254,500
State and Local Law Enforcement Assistance				
Court Appointed Special Advocate (CASA)	12,425	4,500	6,000	6,000
Child Abuse Training for Judicial Personnel	2,071	—	—	—
Children Exposed to Violence	—	10,000	13,000	8,000
State and Local Subtotal	14,496	14,500	19,000	14,000
TOTAL OJJDP:	359,779	277,000	298,500	268,500

[a]EUDL is the Enforcing Underage Drinking Laws Program.
SOURCE: Presentation to the committee, *Overview of OJJDP's Mission and Budget,* by Robert Listenbee and Janet Chiancone, January 22, 2014.

The 2013 NRC report noted that funds to support the Formula Grants Program dropped from two-thirds of OJJDP's budget in its early years to less than one-fifth of its budget in 2010 and that funding for JABG declined from 1999 to 2010 to one-sixth of its original appropriation (see Figure 3-2). That report articulated how declines in funding for OJJDP's formula and categorical grant programs reduced the resources that could be provided to states to address their own needs and limited OJJDP's capacity to influence improvements within juvenile justice systems.

> As the number of appropriated carve-outs continued to rise, OJJDP's portfolio was increasingly shaped by congressional priorities, and its ability to support the agency's original mission declined. . . . By 2008, the budget for its combined state formula and block grant programs dropped to one-third of OJJDP's total budget.
>
> (National Research Council, 2013, pp. 286-287)

> . . . funding available to support juvenile justice improvements by state and local governments. . . steadily declined by 83 percent from 1999 to 2010 in constant 2010 dollars. The reason for this decline is the dramatic decline in funding available through JABG since 2003 as well as the increase in appropriated carve-outs under Title II and Title V (e.g., Enforcing Underage Drinking, Tribal Youth Program, mentoring) and earmarked programs. . . .
>
> (National Research Council, 2013, pp. 308-309)

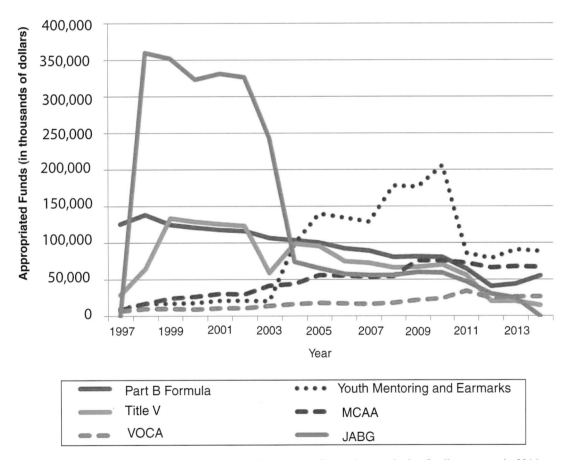

FIGURE 3-2 Trends in Office of Juvenile Justice and Delinquency Prevention continuing funding streams in 2014 constant dollars, 1997-2014.
SOURCE: Committee generated, data provided by Office of Juvenile Justice and Delinquency Prevention.
NOTE: JABG = Juvenile Accountability Block Grant; MCAA = Missing Children Assistance Act; VOCA = Victims of Child Abuse.

> The increase in funds directed at mentoring programs comes at a price. . . . Because funds to support OJJDP's hallmark state formula and block grants are declining, OJJDP is constrained from helping states and localities with other interventions that may better fit their local needs for preventing delinquency. Mentoring is but one intervention. Research has shown that it takes a succession of effective experiences (or interventions) for adolescents to develop into prosocial adults. No single program can serve all youth or incorporate every feature of positive developmental environments (National Research Council and Institute of Medicine, 2002). Therefore, excessive resources in one program, like mentoring, do a disservice to the juvenile justice field more generally and to state, local, and tribal jurisdictions more specifically by overriding or ignoring their efforts to assess their own identified needs and efforts.
>
> (National Research Council, 2013, pp. 313-314)

Little has changed since 2010. OJJDP continues to be allocated funds and responsibility for programs that are only loosely connected to the juvenile justice system. Most important, as Figure 3-2 shows, OJJDP has a declining pot of discretionary funds that can be directed specifically at juvenile justice system improvement. Formula Grants Program funds have been cut in half since 2005, and the JABG Program, a major source of system improvement funding from 1998 to 2004, was zeroed out in 2014. Even in the area of local grants for delinquency prevention, the total Title V funding is less than a quarter of what it was in 2010. As funding has decreased in most grant program areas, concern has been expressed by juvenile justice practitioners that spreading the funding out to multiple program areas and grantees may have the unintended consequence of reducing the impact that the agency can have in achieving its mission.[4]

Declining funds in combination with appropriation carve-outs have diminished the flexibility and reach of OJJDP's research portfolio and its training and technical assistance capacity. The 2002 reauthorization of JJDPA amended Title II to provide authority to the OJJDP administrator to oversee research, evaluation, training, technical assistance, and information dissemination (Title II, Part D).[5] However, funds for Part D were only appropriated in fiscal 2004 and 2005 and discontinued thereafter. Thus, OJJDP relies on a small percentage of its categorical and formula grant funds that can be set aside for training and technical assistance and research as related to the respective topic area. The set-asides through Title II funding streams could be directed at system reform and improvements, given the broad nature of the programs. Unfortunately, in recent years much of this funding has been carved out in appropriations for juvenile mentoring projects; therefore, the set-asides for training and technical assistance and research under this carve-out must be applied toward mentoring.[6] The committee finds it quite disturbing that appropriations for mentoring programs in 2014 exceeded OJJDP's total funding for Part B Formula Grants for states and Title V local delinquency prevention. As noted above, mentoring is just one kind of intervention; whereas funding through the Formula Grants Program and Title V local delinquency prevention can be directed toward other types of interventions, which may be more appropriate to reform in a given jurisdiction.

The agency reported to the committee that it takes a two-pronged approach to planning its research agenda (which includes basic research as well as evaluations and statistical data collections).[7] First, OJJDP uses set-asides from formula funding to support research directly focused on the juvenile justice system and system-involved youths. Given that appropriations for the Formula Grants Program are declining, the agency has directed available funds toward sustaining some of its core research programs such as field-initiated research and evaluation, statistical data analyses, and its model programs guide. Second, OJJDP supports additional research using the directed program funds; this portfolio focuses on delinquency prevention and victimization, although a small proportion of these projects also relate to justice system issues. With directed funding (see Table 3-1), the agency has been able

---

[4]Presentation to the committee by the Advocacy panelists on February 14, 2014. See Appendix A for a list of speakers and interviews.

[5]The 2013 NRC report (p. 311) notes "[t]he original JJDPA of 1974 established the National Institute for Justice and Delinquency Prevention (NIJJDP) within OJJDP to conduct research and evaluation, development and review of standards, training, and collection and dissemination of information. A research institute of significant size and stature never materialized.... The 2002 reauthorization of JJDPA amended Title II to eliminate NIJJDP and provide authority directly to the OJJDP administrator to oversee research, training, technical assistance, and information dissemination."

[6]Presentation to the committee, *Overview of OJJDP's Mission and Budget,* by Robert Listenbee and Janet Chiancone, January 22, 2014. See also H.R. 3547, Omnibus Appropriations Act, 2014, 128 STAT 60.

[7]Presentation to the committee, *Overview of OJJDP's Training and Technical Assistance and Research,* by Brecht Donoghue, January 22, 2014.

to sponsor research on tribal youths, drug courts, mentoring, youth and community-based violence prevention, gangs, underage drinking laws enforcement, missing and exploited children, and children exposed to violence.

OJJDP's portfolio of training and technical assistance is similar to its research portfolio in that directed funding streams are heavily focused on delinquency prevention and child victimization, as opposed to the juvenile justice system and system-involved youths. However, OJJDP has been able to stretch its limited budget for training and technical assistance across a broad set of issues. The agency reported to the committee that it had 65 different training and technical assistance projects. Most of these are specific to a grant or a program, but some are request driven.[8]

The committee heard from constituents that they have substantial needs for training and technical assistance that OJJDP is unable to meet.[9] OJJDP reports it currently funds training and technical assistance projects at about $50 million per year.[10] As noted in the 2013 NRC report, about 80 percent of this is dedicated to programs outside the scope of juvenile justice system improvement (e.g., victims of child abuse and missing and exploited children). Remaining funds are spread across assistance for a broad set of topic areas. The current approach to training or technical assistance is not well suited to deliver the kind of transformation OJJDP is hoping to achieve. It spreads resources in a manner described to the committee as "a mile wide and an inch deep."[11]

A key recommendation in the 2013 NRC report was that federal policy makers should restore OJJDP's capacity to support juvenile justice system improvement through reauthorization, appropriations, and funding flexibility (National Research Council, 2013, p. 328) based upon an analysis of the budget and appropriations that is relevant today:

> [N]umerous carve-outs and earmarks have diminished the capacity of OJJDP's authorized programs—particularly its state formula/block grant programs, mandate to coordinate federal efforts, nonearmarked research and data collection, and technical assistance—to carry out the core requirements of the JJDPA (National Research Council, 2013, p. 308).

To realize greater impact, it may be necessary to further target appropriations on reform of the juvenile justice system and implementation of the hallmarks for that reform (see discussion in Chapter 2). OJJDP currently has authority to provide a range of functions in two statutory domains: delinquency prevention and juvenile justice system improvement. However, its current program portfolio is unbalanced, with the majority of its recent funding resources directed at a single type of intervention: mentoring.

As an approach to building resiliency, mentoring has presented numerous positive effects such as improved academic performance and increased social competence. However, the evidence is less clear about the relationship to delinquency prevention (the agency's mandated function) or the characteristics of youths that benefit most from mentoring (National Research Council, 2013, p. 432). And yet, OJJDP is required to support mentoring for tribal youths, sexually exploited children, youths with disabilities, and youths in military families, regardless of whether there is evidence for (1) the likelihood of the mentored population engaging in delinquent behavior, (2) any benefit from mentoring for those populations, or (3) any connection to preventing delinquency in those populations (National Research Council, 2013, p. 434).

As illustrated in Figure 3-2 and noted in the 2013 report, "the increase in funds directed at mentoring programs comes at a price... Because funds to support OJJDP's hallmark state formula and block grants are declining, OJJDP is constrained from helping states with other interventions that may better fit their local needs for preventing delinquency" (National Research Council, 2013, p. 313). Further, as the only federal agency specifically mandated to assist the states in improving their juvenile justice systems (P.L. 93-415, 42 U.S.C. §5601 *et seq*; also see National Research Council, 2013, p. 281), when the agency's ability to support systemic activities is reduced there are few, if any, alternative sources of assistance. The committee envisions a rebalancing of OJJDP's appropriations to reflect

---

[8]Ibid.

[9]Presentation to the committee by the Legal panelists on February 13, 2014. See Appendix A for a list of speakers and interviews.

[10]Presentation to the committee, *Overview of OJJDP's Training and Technical Assistance and Research,* by Brecht Donoghue, January 22, 2014.

[11]Presentation to the committee by the Advocacy panelists on February 14, 2014. See Appendix A for a list of speakers and interviews.

the full range of OJJDP's mandated functions and an increase in flexibility to allow the agency to target resources to the specific needs of the states.

Even if the agency is given greater flexibility in using its funding, its current appropriations do not give it adequate capacity to carry out the activities that were envisioned by Congress in enacting the JJDPA or the critical mission articulated in this report. The answer to that problem is for federal policy makers to increase both the amount and proportion of the agency's appropriation that are available to the agency to carry out its core mission.

Assisting states, localities, and tribal jurisdictions to align their juvenile justice systems and delinquency prevention programs with current best practices and the results of research on adolescent development and implementing developmentally informed policies, programs, and practices should be the agency's top priority under the JJDPA. Any additional responsibilities and authority conferred on the agency should be amply funded so as not to erode the funds needed to carry out support for system improvement. OJJDP's ability to effect change in the juvenile justice field in the foreseeable future will be severely constrained without adequate legislative and budgetary support by federal policy makers. The funds available to OJJDP should be ample enough, and sufficiently flexible, to enable the agency to hire, train, and retain the necessary staff and to provide the demonstration grants, research, and technical assistance needed to support developmentally informed justice system improvement and reforms by states, tribes, and localities.

The above discussion has focused on changes in OJJDP's funding for programs authorized under JJDPA to show that OJJDP has declining discretion and opportunity to support the needs of and provide assistance to states and localities for juvenile justice system improvement, a primary responsibility under the JJDPA. OJJDP currently has the appropriate authorities and tools across a range of function areas through JJDPA to carry out this purpose, but it will at least need greater flexibility in all funding sources within its budget in order to direct resources to systemic reforms, targeted and efficacious programs, and training or technical assistance designed to support states and localities in efforts to reform their juvenile justice systems. The committee emphasizes that it is not saying Congress should not assign OJJDP responsibilities under other statutes. Rather, the committee's position is that these added duties should be funded adequately on their own and should not be accomplished at the expense of the agency's capacity to carry out its responsibility for supporting juvenile justice system improvement.

ENHANCING INTERNAL CAPACITY

A Common Vision

The administrator and executive staff of OJJDP need to present a clear vision and strategy for change within the agency itself, build or expand internal capacity to support the change, and garner external support. In order to facilitate reform within the nation's diverse juvenile justice system, OJJDP needs to persistently communicate a clear vision and strategy for system reform in state, local, and tribal jurisdictions; prioritize resources for achieving reform; and foster relationships necessary to sustain reform.

To begin to support a developmentally oriented juvenile justice system, OJJDP will need to incorporate the vision of a developmental approach outlined in Chapter 2 into all of its operations, partnerships, and functions (including training and technical assistance, demonstration programs, data collection, research, and information dissemination). In presentations to the committee, the agency reported that all employees have become familiar with the 2013 NRC report and each of the guiding principles (see guiding principles box in Appendix B).[12] It is notable that in 2013-2014 the OJJDP administrator and staff have presented at numerous conferences on the importance of a developmental approach. However, more work needs to occur to bring about changes in the organizational culture and to fully integrate the hallmarks of a developmental approach into OJJDP's grant making and engagement with the juvenile justice field.

In the committee's view, OJJDP's main challenge is to align programs, activities, and staff operations with facilitating juvenile justice system improvement, given that available funding (and resulting programs and operations) have leaned heavily toward delinquency prevention. Changing an institution takes time and persistence and

---

[12]Presentation to the committee, *Overview of OJJDP's Mission and Budget,* by Robert Listenbee and Janet Chiancone, January 22, 2014.

requires a concerted effort to align the organizational culture with a new vision. Part of this investment is necessary to inspire agency staff to embrace the change. Research has identified the following stages of individuals' acceptance during an institutional change (Barnard and Stoll, 2010): (1) employees are unaware that change is needed or intended and are operating to maintain the status quo; (2) employees are resistant and/or uninformed because they have yet to understand the rationale for and the scope of the change and how it will affect them; and eventually (3) employees are accepting of and committed to new policies and practices and the new status quo.

For each stage of resistance/acceptance, communication and support during a period of change should be tailored to the extent possible (Wiggins, 2008/2009). To make decisions on such communication and support, leaders and managers implementing the change should have an understanding of existing, as well as changing, structures, personnel, and culture within the organization (Barnard and Stoll, 2010). One strategy for reducing resistance, recognized in the literature, is to involve employees in the discussions and decisions about the process for implementing changes (Denhardt and Denhardt, 1999; Poister and Streib, 1999; Warwick, 1975).

Recent transformation in the organization and priorities of the Federal Bureau of Investigation (from investigation of federal crimes to intelligence and information gathering to prevention of terrorism), following the terrorist attacks of September 11, 2001, provides an example of how a federal agency implements a comprehensive transformation plan—modifying its own policies, priorities, and practices as necessary; hiring or reassigning staff members with appropriate skills and characteristics; and conducting appropriate staff training—to align and build momentum for successful and sustained transformation (U.S. Department of Justice, 2004; U.S. General Accounting Office, 2003). Once embraced by its organizational culture and implemented in policies, procedures, and practices, a clear vision can continue as a guiding philosophy for OJJDP regardless of subsequent leadership changes.

Staff Training and Curriculum

Efforts are needed to support staff development aimed at gaining the knowledge needed to implement OJJDP's statutory functions so that staff can lead adoption of the desired changes in the juvenile justice system. OJJDP should strive to ensure that each of its divisions is well staffed with trained professionals skilled in the areas needed to guide a strategic reform effort based on a developmental approach. An important step in the agency's strategic effort to remake itself should be to initiate and sustain an agency-wide training activity designed to inform all professional staff about advances in developmental science and their implications for juvenile justice system improvement. The purpose should be to ensure that all staff become and remain current in their knowledge and skills. There will need to be OJJDP staff skilled in working with appropriate decision makers, researchers, and experienced system improvement practitioners in jurisdictions, to help them understand how to achieve desired outcomes. As discussed earlier, many of these jurisdictions are trying to apply a developmental approach to reform of their systems.

A training curriculum will need to be developed that can provide guidance and best practice approaches to OJJDP staff, training and technical assistance providers, and ultimately the juvenile justice field. The curriculum will need to recognize and incorporate the current science of adolescent development and demonstrate methods for applying best practices at each of the key decision points in the juvenile justice system. This is best accomplished through the creation of an external transition advisory group to work with OJJDP leadership and identified staff as part of a transition or change management team. Through this collaborative approach to curriculum development, the best available knowledge, skills, content, length, and learning styles can be incorporated in the context of OJJDP culture and its training and contracting processes, as well as being disseminated to the range of stakeholders in the juvenile justice field.

The best model for such development can be found in best practices employed by a number of experienced universities and certified training institutes. These practices include but are not limited to a course introduction and map; various learning modules that consist of objectives, content presentations and materials; topic assessment/evaluation; and topic discussion opportunities. The course content should cover topics such as the history of the juvenile court and juvenile justice system, including racial disparities; the history and current statutory authority of OJJDP; the best available research on adolescent development, including the relation between brain development and behavior; the hallmarks of a developmental approach to juvenile justice reform (see Box 3-3 and Chapter 2);

BOX 3-3
Hallmarks of the Developmental Approach to Juvenile Justice

1. Accountability Without Criminalization
2. Alternatives to Justice System Involvement
3. Individualized Response Based on Assessment of Needs and Risks
4. Confinement Only When Necessary for Public Safety
5. A Genuine Commitment to Fairness
6. Sensitivity to Disparate Treatment
7. Family Engagement

SOURCE: Committee generated (see Chapter 2).

---

the key components of system change; and strategic partners with whom OJJDP will work to achieve effective implementation of such reforms (see discussion in Chapter 5).

The examples shown in Box 3-4, which feature two key decision points in the juvenile justice system, begin to demonstrate the opportunities that exist for OJJDP—once it has strengthened its internal capacity—to reform the juvenile justice system through the implementation of training and technical assistance that address key decision makers within the system and present methods to apply science-based knowledge about adolescent behavior. OJJDP staff and the agency need to be positioned to use their knowledge of adolescent development to inform the goals and outcomes for the decision makers in the juvenile justice system. This should be accomplished by first ensuring that OJJDP staff internally achieve an expert understanding of the hallmarks of a developmental approach, the research implications for treatment of youths, and the best approaches for appropriately responding to youths, and then using that knowledge to shape the training and technical assistance OJJDP provides. In addition, OJJDP can consider using the Intergovernmental Personnel Act Mobility Program, which provides for the temporary assignment of personnel between the federal government and state and local governments, colleges and universities, Indian tribal governments, federally funded research and development centers, or other eligible organizations. OJJDP also can enter into interagency agreements for the accomplishment of mutual objectives (see Chapter 5).

Recommendation 3-1: OJJDP should develop a staff training curriculum based on the hallmarks of a developmental approach to juvenile justice reform. With the assistance of a team of external experts, it should implement the training curriculum on an ongoing basis and train, assign, or hire staff to align its capabilities with the skills and expertise needed to carry out a developmentally oriented approach to juvenile justice reform.

MAKING SYSTEM REFORM A PRIORITY

Rethinking Training and Technical Assistance

The OJJDP National Training and Technical Assistance Center has published the Core Performance Standards for Training, Technical Assistance and Evaluation to promote consistency, quality, and effective practice in the planning, coordination, delivery, and evaluation of training and technical assistance. For example, these standards for provision of technical assistance outline all documentation that must be received before responding to a request, provide questions for conducting a needs assessment, provide a checklist for developing a comprehensive technical assistance plan, describe how to select a technical assistance provider that is most likely to be able to deliver appropriate information to the target audience, and outline elements of a comprehensive written final report. Although

---

BOX 3-4
Training Curriculum Decision Point Examples

The referral/intake decision is almost universally driven by the statutory requirement of determination of legal sufficiency (or probable cause) that a youth committed a codified offense(s). In the majority of jurisdictions across the country, this decision is frequently followed by a routine next step that involves petitioning the court to formally hear the matter. While there have been advances in the use of diversion and other alternative response opportunities created at this decision point, many jurisdictions only consider legal sufficiency before processing a petition and setting the matter for a court hearing.

Upon receipt and establishment of legal sufficiency, Newton County (Georgia) Juvenile Court has inserted a step that includes an intake staffer that considers additional background information from multiple sources (family, relevant other youth-serving agencies, etc.) prior to determining the most appropriate next process step (St. George, 2011). This step is deliberately intended to explore opportunities to incorporate knowledge derived from developmental science into the treatment plan for the adolescent. This may include simply diverting the adolescent back to the community without services if the level of risk for future offending and need for services are low.

A second example involves the pre-disposition decision by the court. On adjudication of a delinquent offense, many jurisdictions routinely consider only the information available to the court at the time of the adjudication. A much smaller percentage of cases is referred to the probation services department for the preparation of a pre-sentence or pre-disposition report. Combining adjudicatory and dispositional proceedings frequently provides limited or no opportunity to incorporate a developmental approach into an effective intervention plan. Forfeiting the opportunity to adequately incorporate sufficient background developmental information (including validated screening and assessment for dynamic risk factors) in a deliberate and comprehensive manner into the report to the court often results in an array of accountability provisions and court orders without the balance of considering potential contributors to the behavior (National Research Council, 2013, pp.139-181). There are many reasons proffered for this practice (time constraints, workforce resources, federal and state laws precluding exchange of information, etc.), but the failure to account for the developmental aspects in routine practice frequently results in technical violations of the court order and unwanted recidivism.

---

these standards describe the building blocks for understanding technical assistance, they provide little guidance regarding mechanisms and techniques for providing and receiving effective technical assistance.

A clear definition, purpose statement, and vision for technical assistance are needed to use this tool effectively for reform in the states. A valuable set of principles has been compiled in the article, "Providing and Receiving Technical Assistance: Lessons Learned from the Field" (Soler et al., 2013). These lessons reflect important experiences from the technical assistance providers in the MacArthur Foundation's Models for Change initiative and their relationship with the states and local jurisdictions with whom they partnered over the past decade. Lessons from this engagement could guide OJJDP in developing a new approach to technical assistance provided in support of reform efforts:

- The need for technical assistance should be sharply aligned with the reform goals of the jurisdiction.
- Providers should establish clear boundaries on the technical assistance being provided, as well as an exit strategy.
- Providers of both training and technical assistance should be required to demonstrate mastery of the developmental approach; they must develop capacity not only to deliver a training curriculum but also to understand and be responsive to the needs of states, localities, and tribal jurisdictions in implementing system reforms.

- A written training and technical assistance work plan should have concrete objectives, strategies to be employed, desired outcomes, measures of progress, individuals responsible for each activity, and timelines for completion.
- Jurisdictions and technical assistance providers should collect and analyze data necessary to assess the effectiveness of efforts to provide a solution to the technical assistance request.
- Technical assistance providers should offer concrete examples of other jurisdictions and facilitate inter-jurisdictional connections.

It is clear from these lessons that system reforms require intensive and sustained engagement. Each juvenile justice system is different, and each has different strengths and weaknesses. Given the unique features of each jurisdiction, the duration and intensity of technical assistance should match the actual need for support to build capacity and achieve objectives.

Long-term, intensive assistance has been arguably absent from the OJJDP approach in recent years. In addition, OJJDP's reliance on a pay scale for designated technical assistance providers that had not increased since the 1990s has undercut the agency's ability to partner with many of the best and most knowledgeable juvenile justice experts (Office of Juvenile Justice and Delinquency Prevention, 2014).[13] Some of the OJJDP-approved providers are not viewed in the field as having expertise in the areas for which they are approved by OJJDP to deliver training and technical assistance. For example, in the area of family engagement, some providers lack staff expertise as a family member of a system-involved youth and have not transparently consulted families impacted by the system (i.e., system-involved families or legacy families) in the development of resource materials.

A notable requirement of the JJDPA is that training and technical assistance partnership grants may be made "only to public and private agencies, organizations, and individuals that have experience in providing such technical assistance" (P.L. 93-415, 42 U.S.C. §5601 (Sec. 221)(b)(2)). OJJDP should strive to identify training and technical assistance providers that have the expertise to meet the needs of states and localities. In this current period of reform, this will require working knowledge of the hallmarks of a developmental approach to reform discussed in Chapter 2. Providers must be receptive to and skilled in analyzing the nuances of a client's juvenile justice system so that a clear plan can be developed. Execution of that plan needs support as well, so multiyear commitments may be needed. In addition, if the entity requesting technical assistance does not have robust data collection and reporting systems, that deficiency must be addressed as a threshold matter or as part of the first step in establishing the reform effort. Data should be used to establish baselines and track progress (see discussion on administrative data later in this chapter).

While the approaches to technical assistance vary, the lessons from the provision of technical assistance through foundation-led efforts such as the Models for Change initiative and the Juvenile Detention Alternatives Initiative are instructive as OJJDP embarks upon a new and more strategic approach to delivering training and technical assistance. Providers will also need to be able to develop or access learning networks[14] to facilitate interjurisdictional connections, sharing of information, and imparting lessons learned. The training curriculum discussed earlier should also be modified to train providers. Such preparation for providers and a framework for providing training and technical assistance to states and localities based on a system improvement model are set forth in greater detail in Chapter 4.

General Grant Making

As with many government grant-making agencies, OJJDP has the competing goals of funding innovative and promising programs while remaining vigilant to the risk of waste, fraud, and abuse in awarding and overseeing grants (U.S. Department of Justice, 2009a). OJJDP once enjoyed a reputation for pioneering grant making in partnership with grantees while upholding the highest standards of integrity. That reputation has suffered in recent

---

[13]OJJDP's pay scale for technical assistance providers was changed in May 2014 (increased to $650 per day).

[14]"Learning community," "learning network," or "community of practice" are terms to describe a group of people who intentionally share information and experiences to learn from each other and to accelerate the learning curve of the members (Wenger et al., 2002).

years, likely due to the pressures resulting from the scrutiny of the agency's 2007 grant awards combined with a lack of leadership and strategic vision (U.S. Department of Justice, 2009b).

Many in the field see OJJDP as overly focused on grant and compliance monitoring, with staff largely viewed as grant auditors rather than potential partners in reform efforts.[15] OJJDP's role in enforcing compliance with the core protections from the JJDPA appears to consume significant staff resources, despite the fact that compliance rates are in the mid-90th percentiles and the agency has limited ability to bring the few noncompliant states into compliance (Office of Juvenile Justice and Delinquency Prevention, 2012). Similarly, the resources spent on monitoring grant activities seem to this committee to be outsized in relation to the gains to the agency, the grantees, or the field.

While it is necessary, of course, to ensure that awarded monies are spent on projected activities and services, the committee is convinced that this function can be served much more efficiently. OJJDP should strive to establish a better balance between grant monitoring and system reform activities by re-examining the monitoring systems to identify ways to ensure compliance that are less resource-intensive. The agency demonstrated this balancing previously, and the possibilities include (1) a random audit of representative samples with in-depth reviews of selected programs, with monitoring focused on outcomes rather than process; (2) a rotating schedule of full reviews with monitoring of remediation plans in the intervening years; or (3) contracting out the monitoring function.

Recommendation 3-2: OJJDP should establish a better balance between grant monitoring and system reform efforts by examining more efficient ways to monitor grants and compliance with the core protections from the JJDPA.

In addition, OJJDP resources have been reduced but the priorities of OJJDP have remained broad, thus spreading resources too thinly across too many activities. OJJDP can restore its reputation for strategic grant making—while still supporting the needs in the field—by concentrating the focus of its grants on the hallmarks of a developmental approach. The committee notes that OJJDP previously achieved this type of balance in its work through the Comprehensive Strategy for Serious, Violent and Chronic Juvenile Offenders (hereafter, the Comprehensive Strategy) and adopting a similar approach would support a developmental focus across the agency's prevention and intervention activities. OJJDP would also be well served by re-examining many of the tools and resources created in past years such as "cciTools," which was created for federal agency staff[16] and contains useful generic grant-making resources designed to support system reform activities.

Demonstration Grants

Under Sections 261 and 262 of the JJDPA, OJJDP has the authority to develop, in partnership with a select number of states, demonstration or pilot grant programs that could be designed to improve the routine use of the hallmarks of a developmental approach. The JJDPA authorizes OJJDP to support units of local governments and other public and private agencies and organizations to develop, test, and demonstrate promising initiatives and to provide technical assistance to those entities. Extensive, sustained, high-quality technical assistance through partnerships with national organizations will be needed to plan and implement these system reforms. (See Chapter 4 for discussion on training and technical assistance and Chapter 5 for discussion of partnering with national organizations to provide such training and technical assistance.)

OJJDP will need to explore with its federal agency partners ways to blend or leverage available federal, state, and local funds to support these demonstration grants. This could be accomplished by providing greater flexibility in allowable uses of existing federal financing; dedicating a share of, or creating a preference within, an existing federal program; creating exemptions (or waivers) for certain state or federal funding restrictions based on a link to the results sought, such as the state match, program eligibility requirements, or timelines in existing federal programs; and pooling federal funding by bundling several programs under the initiative. (For further discussion

---

[15]Presentation to the committee by the Legal, Advocacy, and State Advisory Group panelists on February 13 and 14, 2014. See Appendix A for a list of speakers and interviews.

[16]For more information, see http://www.ccitoolsforfeds.org [May 14, 2014].

of leveraging funding streams, see Chapter 5.) In addition, OJJDP will need to explore public/private partnerships with a foundation or consortium of foundations to create flexible funding that can be made available to states, counties, cities, or tribes that are selected to participate in the demonstration. OJJDP's goal for demonstration grants would be to provide replicable guidance for state, local, and tribal jurisdictions across the country, based upon the documented experiences and achievements of these pilot jurisdictions, while building requirements for reforms into future grant making.

As noted above and in the 2013 NRC report, a signature program of OJJDP that evolved more than a decade ago—the Comprehensive Strategy—is illustrative of OJJDP's past efforts to support research-based demonstration programs combined with technical assistance efforts that focus on both systemic reform and evidence-based programmatic interventions. The Comprehensive Strategy, utilizing the best available research from what commonly became known as risk and protective factor science, brought together an array of youth-serving system professionals in a community to frame a proactive system response to juvenile delinquency. The systemic change approach of the Comprehensive Strategy supported development and implementation of a continuum of programs aimed at targeted prevention, early intervention, and graduated sanctions at every key decision point of the juvenile justice system. Jurisdictions from across the country engaged in this strategy with support and guidance provided by OJJDP.

IMPROVING DATA AND PROMOTING USEFUL RESEARCH

The 2013 NRC report expressed concern about the lack of consistent data on numerous juvenile justice issues and recent reform efforts. These limited data capacities in juvenile justice have challenged the field for many years, and the current lack of extensive data is largely the legacy of limited and unfocused resources committed to the issue of juvenile delinquency throughout the federal government. The goals outlined in the 2013 NRC report increase the challenges. Making significant advances in promoting accountability, adopting effective interventions, and increasing fairness all require more empirically sound measurement and management strategies than those now used in juvenile justice. Many current data systems at the federal and local levels are inadequate to this task. Much needs to be done to integrate advances in technology, data management, and analysis into state juvenile justice systems. Other sectors have made the effort and have reaped benefits.

OJJDP can and should take a leadership role in improving data quality and research in juvenile justice. The agency has taken such a role in the past (National Research Council, 2013, Chapter 10) and can build on its own accomplishments. In this current period, OJJDP can focus its efforts in these areas on the goal of reforming juvenile justice practice and policy. OJJDP can serve as a central coordinating point for information about innovations, promising approaches, and useful strategies. Perhaps more importantly, it can serve as a motivating force for improvements in data collection and management as well as research in juvenile justice. It can fulfill this vision of fostering innovation in two ways: (1) supporting and guiding upgrades to federal, state, local, and tribal administrative data systems; and (2) identifying and supporting collaborative research projects that capitalize on OJJDP's program activities and those of other agencies.

Improving Administrative Data Collection and Management

Available data on juvenile justice practice is highly variable across states and localities. This variability makes it difficult to identify generalizable knowledge, mount sound reviews or studies of specific practice or policy approaches, and promote collaboration across localities regarding new practices. OJJDP could advance the field considerably by putting more effort into the development of broadly applicable methods for collecting uniform information. This could be done with consultation regarding administrative software development, efforts to increase uniformity regarding data collection methods, and activities aimed at collaborative problem solving across localities.

Many localities develop their own information management systems or contract with businesses to develop such systems, largely de novo.[17] As part of its leadership role, OJJDP could promote infrastructure and data element definitions that would both modernize existing systems and allow comparisons across localities. To promote more systemwide consistency, OJJDP could provide model formats or specifications for information management systems as well as consultation regarding the implementation of such systems. Such guidelines could be produced from ongoing consultations with localities about their successes and challenges in implementing data management systems, as well as from meetings and shared activities among data management professionals in different localities. In addition, information and expertise about data organization and management could be gathered systematically from other agencies in the Office of Justice Programs (the National Institute of Justice and Bureau of Justice Statistics) and other federal agencies with histories of mounting multisite studies requiring consistent data collection and integration (for example, the National Institutes of Health). Attention will need to be paid to the sensitive nature of juvenile justice data in order to safeguard the confidentiality of individuals' data. Regular work groups and conferences coordinated by OJJDP could provide the necessary formats for increasing the consistency and quality of information available across state and local jurisdictions.

These efforts will have to be incremental, involving a limited set of localities at a time; it will take a great deal of effort to reach consensus among localities about processes and definitions. At the same time, the payoff from these efforts would be considerable. Improved and more uniform data systems and data collection methods across localities would make cross-site comparisons and projects possible. Jurisdictions would be able to assess the viability of improvements to their systems if they have useful and comparable data to measure recidivism rates or other key youth outcomes during and beyond periods of system supervision. If localities reached some consensus on the definition of particular operational features of their local juvenile justice systems (e.g., what constitutes a technical probation violation), they could then confidently compare outcomes across localities. This could lead to more broadly applicable knowledge, rather than singular "demonstrations" that often fail replication. In addition, natural experiments could be mounted in which different practices are used in regular practice across multiple jurisdictions and comparable data are collected at each site. Attaining an acceptable level of uniformity across localities is the necessary first step toward these types of activities. OJJDP is the only agency that is positioned to promote the needed consistency across localities.

Recommendation 3-3: OJJDP should take a leadership role in local, state, and tribal jurisdictions with respect to the development and implementation of administrative data systems by providing model formats for system structure, standards, and common definitions of data elements. OJJDP should also provide consultation on data systems as well as opportunities for sharing information across jurisdictions.

Supporting Collaborative, Applied Research with a Developmental Focus

Three orientations have dominated OJJDP's data analysis and research efforts over recent years. The first has been a concern with documenting the functions of the system nationally, such as collecting and analyzing information on numbers of juveniles arrested, petitioned, or sent to institutions in different localities. Much of this work has been done by the National Center for Juvenile Justice, interpreting and integrating reports of system processing figures obtained from states or localities. The second major orientation has been toward the identification of individual programs that "work" to prevent or reduce delinquency among the program participants (measured almost exclusively by re-arrest data). The programs that work are compiled in the Model Programs Guide (now merged with CrimeSolutions.gov [http://www.crimesolutions.gov], the website sponsored by the Office of Justice Programs for information on criminal justice program effectiveness). The third has been the funding of selected research projects regarding factors related to the development or continuation of delinquency (e.g., the Causes and Correlates of Delinquency studies, Pathways to Desistance study, gang research, and research on effects of mentoring programs).

---

[17]Performance-based standards, as discussed in Chapter 2 and in the 2013 NRC report, provide an example of performance measures for facility safety, behavior management, health, mental health and substance abuse services, case management and reentry planning, programming and education, and connections to family and community resources (National Research Council, 2013).

There is much to be said for the value of these activities. Collecting and reporting data on systems regularities serve important management purposes. First, they indicate whether there are discernible trends over time that might inform where resources should be directed (e.g., how much of an increase is there in violent offenses by females?). These trends might indicate changes in actual offending behavior that need to be investigated or shifts in processing patterns that deserve attention. Second, these figures can provide benchmarks for localities, telling them whether their systems are operating differently from most other localities. If, for instance, a locality's rate of institutional placement is well above that seen in other comparable sites, local administrators can examine their practices to see whether there are changes they might make to reduce this rate. Providing information about program effectiveness will give leads to practitioners about possible intervention strategies and to policy makers about ways to set funding and service priorities. Research on developmental patterns of delinquency and effects of particular factors on continued delinquency at different ages provides basic information needed to generate informed interventions and policies.

These activities alone do not, however, adequately promote a developmental perspective on juvenile justice. Data on system regularities mainly help in management decisions about how to structure the processes for handling adolescents who come to the attention of the system, but they contain little information on outcomes from intervention. Identifying and certifying programs as "working" with particular groups of adolescents promotes the idea that certain interventions or prevention programs have a universal applicability, with little attention paid to the relevant developmental outcomes connected with involvement in juvenile justice services. These approaches do not address whether the system is effective at preparing youths for becoming productive adults or whether youths have achieved critical developmental milestones that the juvenile justice system could be promoting.

OJJDP will need to promote expanded data collection to capture the effects of particular juvenile justice practices or policies on development and to understand developmental influences on the effectiveness of practices and policies. There would also need to be an emphasis on measuring outcomes beyond arrest or return to an institution and on requiring more data about system-involved adolescents from systems outside of juvenile justice. As noted in Chapter 3 of the 2013 NRC report, the systems affecting delinquent adolescents are multilayered, decentralized, and variable across localities. Juvenile justice operations intersect with schools, families, law enforcement officials, child welfare professionals, and social service providers to prevent adolescent crime, intervene with juveniles who offend, and promote public safety and justice. This reality implies that juvenile justice agencies must build collaborative relationships with these other social agencies to paint an accurate picture of how an adolescent's life unfolds and to understand how juvenile justice involvement fits into this process.

Thus, research done in conjunction with schools, families, and social service providers is necessary to examine factors beyond just court intervention. Such work is best done in a collaborative fashion. OJJDP and state or local juvenile justice agencies need the cooperation and viewpoints from system partners (e.g., school professionals, social service providers) in conceptualizing, implementing, and interpreting research regarding efforts to prevent or respond to adolescent offending. Research on these questions is simply too complicated and expensive for individual federal, state, or local juvenile justice agencies to address on their own, across all the points of juvenile justice processing or localities: for OJJDP, this means mounting collaborative research projects with other federal agencies and promoting collaborative efforts at the state and local levels. These efforts would focus on specific and delimited questions about how the juvenile justice system interacts with school, families, and service providers to promote delinquency prevention and intervention efforts that coordinate resources among these sectors to reduce entry into the juvenile justice system, limit that involvement, or prevent re-offending. To determine how to do this, OJJDP can pursue three activities to develop a focused research portfolio to support system reform efforts.

First, OJJDP can identify opportunities to capitalize on its dual functions of funding program and research activities. Unique among Office of Justice Programs' agencies, OJJDP has the joint mandate to fund both program initiatives and research on juvenile justice, delinquency, and prevention. There is considerable potential in integrating these two activities more closely to use program activities as platforms for research, supplementing intervention activities with resources to support applied research and data collection. To do this, OJJDP staff need to be more knowledgeable about research design and the state of delinquency research, but they do not necessarily have to be adept at conducting independent research. Their role would be that of a knowledgeable broker who can identify collaborative opportunities and bring them to fruition. Such research activities can be coordinated with the research-practitioner partnerships and visiting fellow programs. These joint initiatives can identify intervention opportunities to collect data on aspects of adolescent development (e.g., perceptions of deterrence or indicators of perceived fairness) that might mitigate the adjustment of system-involved adolescents. It is the responsibility of OJJDP to capitalize on these possibilities.

Second, OJJDP could use outside scholarly experts on specific content areas to develop research agendas and to help identify collaborative projects that could be pursued with other federal partners (e.g., the National Institute of Child Health and Human Development, National Institute on Drug Abuse, and National Science Foundation) or foundations and academic institutions. OJJDP needs to develop a more focused research portfolio, using adolescent development as an orienting principle. This can be accomplished using ad hoc committees of experts to provide research ideas and expertise about design, measurement, analysis, and interpretation of research results. Limiting research to a few topics and integrating it with OJJDP's own program activities and those of other agencies would produce more in-depth research information on a set of high-priority issues in the field. Such an initiative would be in line with the recommendations of a previous NRC report calling for the increased use of consultants on particular topics in criminal justice agencies in general (National Research Council, 2005). It would also be the first step in moving OJJDP toward a research agenda that focuses on "why" and "how" particular programs or policies work. It would thus be a large step toward a more scientific approach to juvenile justice and delinquency research.

Third, OJJDP could advance research initiatives in the juvenile justice field by promoting data uniformity among researchers. Building comprehensive knowledge about program effects and developmental constructs (e.g., perceptions of fairness) requires consistent measurement of constructs. Currently, measures used to portray constructs or outcomes in research studies vary from investigator to investigator or agency to agency. OJJDP could propose preferred measures for constructs of interest to be used in many evaluations or research projects. Just as the agency now provides information regarding programs with proven records of success in the Model Programs Guide and at CrimeSolutions.gov, it could also provide information about measures with sound psychometric characteristics.

OJJDP's role in promoting uniformity of research measures would largely be to serve as the arbiter of professional opinions and to endorse the use of particular forms of data collection to the field. The agency can lead by setting the standards for the field and creating incentives for others to follow. A limited requirement for uniformity in the data collected could, however, prove useful. OJJDP could provide a list of a few sound instruments for assessing certain commonly measured key constructs (e.g., peer associations). Grantees could be required to use at least one of the instruments on the list, with the option of using others of their choosing in addition to a required instrument. Enforcement of such a practice has been implemented successfully by the Substance Abuse and Mental Health Services Administration, whose approach could provide a useful model. Having consistent data across multiple research studies could lead to consolidations of datasets and would be a major step forward in generating broadly interpretable information.

Recommendation 3-4: OJJDP should focus research efforts toward specific projects related to a developmental perspective on juvenile justice, capitalizing on an integration of its research and program efforts.

OJJDP is poised to make a substantial contribution to the generation of more useful, accessible, and valid information to guide program implementation and policy formulation. However, achieving this possibility will require a reorientation of effort and resources. It requires a federal agency that takes the lead in identifying issues that matter to moving state systems forward; focuses its resources on projects and research that address these issues; coordinates the collection of uniform data; and works collaboratively with outside experts, academic institutions, other federal agencies, and foundations. Moving from a role as a compiler of information about programs or approaches to a promoter of strategic and efficacious practices or policies would have a profound influence on the field. This style of leadership would translate into more consistent data reporting, more informed management, and sounder, more integrated research to inform practice and policy discussions.

DISSEMINATING INFORMATION

The effort to engage in strategic information dissemination will build momentum and sustainability such that the developmental approach to juvenile justice continues as a guiding philosophy regardless of changes in OJJDP's leadership. OJJDP currently has the tools to export knowledge through a variety of technologies and methods. These include but are not limited to: national conferences, training symposia and forums (regional, state, and local), research briefs, newsletters, special topic reports, webcasts and webinars events, special topic meetings and trainings, guiding publications, white papers, toolkits, fact sheets, and other online resources.

OJJDP staff should develop an outreach and deployment strategy beyond the State Advisory Groups to include partner agencies and organizations at the federal level and affiliated national organizations (see Chapters 4 and 5) and to ensure that these key partners understand the basis for reform policies, are aware of the partnership opportunities for improving the juvenile justice system, and assist with the dissemination of this information to the key decision makers within their networks.

Furthermore, OJJDP should hold itself accountable for its efforts to infuse a developmental perspective into its operations. All of OJJDP's activities discussed in this chapter, including information dissemination, better data, relevant research, and training and technical assistance, should promote the implementation of a developmental perspective in juvenile justice. If these activities are not pursued adequately or if they do not have the intended effect, OJJDP should be prepared to change its tactics. This requires that OJJDP develop a strategy to monitor its own activities, set benchmarks, and measure outcomes to determine if it has had the desired effect on the field. OJJDP has to serve as a model for self-monitoring and correction, to promote these activities more broadly in the field.

4

Facilitating Change Within the Jurisdictions

As discussed in Chapter 3, the Office of Juvenile Justice and Delinquency Prevention (OJJDP) has a number of tools available to guide states, localities, and tribal jurisdictions in their implementation of reforms using a developmental approach, including leadership, capacity building, and incentives, all undergirded by existing legal authority. This chapter explores how OJJDP can support training for state leaders, how training and technical assistance should evolve to effectively meet the current needs of jurisdictions, how OJJDP could modify its approach to reducing racial and ethnic disparities within the juvenile justice system based on current research, and how support for demonstration programs could advance juvenile justice reform and fill knowledge gaps. The chapter concludes with a look at reinvestment and realignment strategies that are currently being considered by many states.

FEDERAL LEADERSHIP

During the past 15 years, substantial progress has been made by numerous states and local jurisdictions in embracing and implementing a more developmentally appropriate way of handling youths in the juvenile justice system (National Research Council, 2013, p. 278). Nevertheless, states and localities commonly look to OJJDP for guidance in many areas of governance due to its relative stability within the federal government and a traditional belief that federal agencies maintain a high level of expertise and are positioned to assess successful efforts in the states. Thus, the singular voice of a federal agency is amplified, making it a uniquely effective instrument of change in a highly diverse system. Using this platform, OJJDP is positioned to spotlight the science of adolescent development and its implications for juvenile justice system improvement and delinquency prevention. The 2013 National Research Council (NRC) report noted overwhelming support from the juvenile justice field for rejuvenated federal leadership (National Research Council, 2013, pp. 317-318); this continues to be true, as this committee heard from all those who presented to it (see Appendix A) of the potential value of federal leadership and commitment to juvenile justice reform.

NURTURING STATE LEADERSHIP

Leadership of reforms based on a developmental approach to juvenile justice reform may come from a variety of places, depending upon the state, local, or tribal jurisdiction. The committee notes that the "prework" required to nurture readiness for reform in a state may take many different forms. It may be launched as a public event championed by a political leader, generated by the momentum from a grassroots movement or more formalized organization, or quietly and strategically led by a determined change agent, often supported by foundation resources ranging from expert consultation to targeted funding. The 2013 NRC report observed (pp. 326-327) that past successful reform efforts have been the result of engaged state leaders and collaborative efforts often led by foundation initiatives. However, the precise vehicle for change—task force, political leader, advocacy organization, or change agent—needs to be based upon the specifics of the jurisdiction.

The Juvenile Justice and Delinquency Prevention Act of 1974 (JJDPA) requires each state to have a State Advisory Group (SAG), which is to be composed of citizens, advocates, and government officials at various levels. SAGs serve several functions, including overseeing juvenile justice grant funds from OJJDP, monitoring the four core requirements, and developing or reviewing 3-year state plans (42 U.S.C. 5633 [Sec. 223]). Given their authority, the SAGs have the potential to become key players in a juvenile justice reform effort, serving as a conduit for the efforts that OJJDP could leverage at the state level. However, the committee understands that currently the SAGs are in varying degrees of readiness to engage in, much less lead, a developmental approach to juvenile justice reform. It has been suggested that approximately one-third of SAGs are in a mature stage of organizational development and are "reform-minded."[1] Many SAG members view their work as focused exclusively on the core protections in the JJDPA, and not all SAGs are effective even at this most basic function.[2]

Given the range of leadership sources, the committee addresses the discussion here both to SAGs and to other "state leaders" to acknowledge the variety of leadership constellations that might exist in a particular jurisdiction. Building the capacity of a SAG, another multistakeholder collaborative body, or even an individual change agent, is one of the fundamental tasks that OJJDP can undertake to foster a developmentally appropriate juvenile justice system. An important component will be to foster involvement of legacy families[3] in the SAGs. The committee agrees with the position of Potter and Brough (2004), who argued that building the capacity of SAGs should be a key component of OJJDP's strategic plan. The committee views OJJDP as having two roles in the capacity building of state leaders: (1) being a reliable resource for guidance and assistance and (2) ensuring that SAGs and support staff are appropriately trained.

The hallmarks of a developmental approach to reform discussed in Chapter 2 include family engagement. Involving families in individual cases improves outcomes for most youths who become involved with the juvenile justice system or other legal authorities; engaging families in the oversight of juvenile justice provides a valuable perspective in planning reform and juvenile justice interventions and treatment. Currently, SAGs do not include legacy families as members, nor do they regularly solicit input from legacy families. OJJDP should support culture and organizational change within the SAGs to create an environment where legacy families are equal and respected members of each SAG. Facilitating active and meaningful participation by youths and families in a SAG may necessitate reimbursements for time off from work, transportation, and other costs necessary for meeting participation.[4] To increase youth and family partnerships as integral SAG participants in juvenile justice reform, OJJDP could encourage the SAGs to establish and support advisory groups of youths and the families of system-involved youths, if such groups are not already in existence.

If SAGs are going to play a key role in the task of reforming a system as complex as a given state's juvenile justice system, they may require political support from the highest levels in their state: the governor, the legislature, the judiciary, or a combination of these. OJJDP could provide guidance for developing strategic approaches and sustaining political support. OJJDP should also facilitate access to fiscal resources, human resources, and tools in order to enable SAGs not only to perform their mandated functions effectively but also to lead system reform efforts. OJJDP also has the opportunity to promote capacity building through a closer and more strategic partnership with the Federal Advisory Committee on Juvenile Justice and the Coalition for Juvenile Justice (see Chapter 5).

---

[1]Discussion with Advocacy and SAG panel to the Committee on a Prioritized Plan to Implement a Developmental Approach in Juvenile Justice Reform, February 13-14, 2014.

[2]Presentation by Marie Williams and Robin Jenkins to the Committee on a Prioritized Plan to Implement a Developmental Approach in Juvenile Justice Reform, February 13, 2014.

[3]"Legacy families" is defined in Chapter 1.

[4]OJJDP may need the authority to authorize the use of administrative funds to support the SAG or may need a source of flexible resources, for example, through a public-private partnership.

Training and technical assistance provided by OJJDP, as discussed below, could be an integral part of a state's reform efforts. SAGs ought to be fully engaged in the training, technical assistance, and consultation provided. They also have responsibility to allocate federal funds for implementation of programs and effective practices that support reform. To be effective in these roles, each SAG member should have a full understanding of adolescent development and the hallmarks of a developmental approach to juvenile justice reform. OJJDP could require SAG members to complete the curriculum discussed in Chapter 3. OJJDP can also provide recommended standards for the hiring and training of staff who serve the SAGs. SAGs require staff with the knowledge and skills necessary to support a collaborative body that is guiding, overseeing, or participating in transformational change. A verification methodology could be developed before acknowledging a state's assurance(s) that its SAG members have each completed the OJJDP curriculum on the developmental approach.[5] OJJDP could also invest in developing the knowledge and skills of SAG members to support the culture and organizational change that could be necessary within each agency, organization, and entity that is part of the juvenile justice system.

Pursuant to the JJDPA, the SAGs are responsible for developing a 3-year plan for addressing delinquency prevention and intervention in their state, including methods for complying with the core protections. The SAGs update these plans annually and submit annual performance reports to OJJDP that describe progress in implementing programs outlined in the original plan (42 U.S.C. §5633, State plans). OJJDP has the opportunity to amend the state plan requirements to include a plan for and progress report on implementing a developmental approach to reform in the state.

Recommendation 4-1: OJJDP should promote the development and strengthening of the State Advisory Groups (SAGs) to be juvenile justice reform leaders by supporting meaningful family and youth engagement, fostering partnerships, delivering strategic training and technical assistance aimed at facilitating reform, and ensuring that SAG members and staff are knowledgeable about the hallmarks of a developmental approach to juvenile justice.

TRAINING AND TECHNICAL ASSISTANCE

The committee envisions a technical assistance framework that provides capacity-building support in two broad categories: tactical and strategic. Tactical forms of technical assistance are specific in focus and short in duration (referred to as Levels 1 and 2 in the framework in Table 4-1). They address a specific activity or support development of a particular skill, such as the development of a risk assessment tool and training on its use. This technical assistance can provide basic information to provide and promote access to up-to-date information and resources.

Strategic technical assistance[6] is more intensive, provided over a long-term horizon, and is better suited for addressing complex issues (referred to as Levels 3, 4, and 5 in the framework in Table 4-1). Strategic technical assistance spans multiple years, and, when it is well executed, it is customized to the local level and decisions are data-driven. In the present context, strategic technical assistance supports overall system reform.

Strategic and tactical technical assistance are both necessary tools for OJJDP to fulfill its mission. The committee recommends a balance of these two categories so that OJJDP can continue providing some of the tactical technical assistance it has been providing while also allocating substantial resources for long-term strategic technical assistance for the implementation of the developmental approach to juvenile justice reform.

Given the expense of a long-term commitment for technical assistance and the scarcity of resources, OJJDP will need to be strategic in deciding which localities or states are eligible to receive assistance. This can be accomplished through a competitive process where OJJDP evaluates applicants through subjective and objective criteria, based on both the excellence of the application and the entity's commitment, readiness, and capacity to engage in reform. Providers of strategic training and technical assistance could be chosen based upon their demonstrated

---

[5]The OJJDP administrator has the statutory authority to approve annual performance reports from each state (P.L. 93-415, 42 U.S.C. §5633, State plans).

[6]Notably, while OJJDP refers to the use of strategic consultation, the committee heard repeatedly from the field that, too often, OJJDP training and technical assistance is inadequate, poorly delivered, and conducted in a "spray and pray" approach. See Appendix A for a list of speakers and interviews.

TABLE 4-1 Capacity Building Through a Training and Technical Assistance Framework

	Type of Engagement	Recipient/Participant	Activity	Provider
TACTICAL	**Level 1. Ongoing**	The juvenile justice field—for general knowledge	Brokering of resources: • Partnering with national organizations • Contracting with providers • Matching providers with grantee(s) based upon (1) demonstration grant status, (2) grantee self-assessment identifying need, (3) demonstrated expertise of provider Dissemination of materials: • Newsletters, reports, Web-based resources	Staff of the agency National partner organizations
TACTICAL	**Level 2. Short-term, infrequent, self-contained**	All grantees, system partners, professionals at all decision points, SAGs—to address a specific, identified need; upon request	Overview trainings without skill building, to raise awareness of an issue or topic: • Trainings • Workshops • Webinars • Computer-based courses	Training organizations National partner organizations
STRATEGIC	**Level 3. Long-term, intensive**	Demonstration site grantees (senior leadership, management, supervisors, staff, partners, providers, SAGs)—to support initiating a reform plan	In depth, customized training for specific skills and to build sustainability: • Multisession training with skill building • Training of trainers • Coaching • Help desk	Expert consultants National partner organizations
STRATEGIC	**Level 4. Continuing, targeted**	Demonstration site grantees (individuals or teams)—to build on reform gains, expand, go to scale	Ongoing support for implementation of new plans, practice, or tasks: • Mentoring (one-on-one, matched teams) • Technical assistance to small groups	Peer-to-peer technical assistance
STRATEGIC	**Level 5. Periodic, field generated**	Cohorts of demonstration sites (individuals or teams)—to sustain reforms, share and streamline lessons learned	Transfer of learning to build in sustainability: • Regional conferences • Topical conferences • Online discussion boards • Social networks	Learning networks/communities Communities of practice

SOURCE: Adapted from Brown et al. (1999); Garet et al. (2001); Grindle and Hilderbrand (1995); O'Donnell et al. (2000); and Ray et al. (2012).

proficiency and experience with systems reform and with the hallmarks of the developmental approach. In addition, OJJDP can identify opportunities to work with federal agency and national organization partners in the delivery of training and technical assistance in a coordinated and strategic approach, as illustrated in the case of community corrections in New York City, described in Box 4-1. (See also Chapter 5.)

Strategic technical assistance, as the committee has explained it here, is not a scientifically validated approach to system reform. A review of the literature turned up no scientifically validated approaches to juvenile justice

---

BOX 4-1
Case Study of a Federal and Locality Partnership

Local corrections agencies struggle with short-term technical assistance provided by federal agencies to achieve the goals of systemic reform, which has raised concerns that such assistance is insufficiently robust. Over the past several years, New York City's Department of Probation (NYCDOP) has received support and technical assistance from experts funded by the Bureau of Justice Assistance (BJA) and the National Institute of Corrections (NIC) to help the organization infuse evidence-based practices throughout its approach. According to a case study (Ziedenberg, 2014), the collaborative partnership of NYCDOP, BJA, and NIC was unique in that the three moved beyond the traditional limitations of federally funded technical assistance by:

- targeting limited federal and local resources over a sustained period of time; and
- identifying and funding technical assistance items "a la carte" through a strategic interchange based on an assessment of NYCDOP's needs and in real time as the reforms unfolded.

BJA and NIC exhibited a high level of cooperation and blended their approaches, maximizing scarce technical assistance resources. The assistance was provided in a timely, flexible, and targeted fashion in partnership with NYCDOP. It was delivered as part of a strategic approach that included funding from philanthropy and local and state government sources. During a time when NYCDOP was coordinating and shepherding several cutting-edge initiatives, the technical assistance provided by BJA and NIC allowed NYCDOP to:

- Survey and assess staff readiness to adopt new practices and map staff strengths and needs;
- Implement and use the Level of Service Inventory-Revised—a validated risk/needs assessment tool that is now being used across all five boroughs;
- Train over 415 staff in restorative justice practices;
- Train 305 staff in community engagement approaches;
- Train 437 staff in motivational interviewing approaches;
- Use cutting-edge training regiments like SOARING 2, an e-learning system created to assist justice professionals in building skills associated with the effective management of clients in the community; and
- Develop a series of communications and staff engagement strategies.

This focused, tailored federal technical assistance, combined with NYCDOP's internal and foundation-funded methods, has enabled the agency to move toward a more evidence-based and developmentally appropriate approach to probation practice. The federal efforts melded so seamlessly with the city's efforts that they became one effort, without being either too shallow to effect the desired outcome or too extensive and costly that they consumed so much of BJA's/NIC's resources as to make this approach impossible to replicate elsewhere.

SOURCE: Ziedenberg (2014).

reform. However, in the committee's collective judgment, the foundation-led initiatives offer compelling examples of how providing an intensive, locally focused, multiyear approach to training and technical assistance is an effective way to achieve system reform in juvenile justice.

Creating tailored assistance will be challenging; each juvenile justice system has different strengths and weaknesses. As noted in Chapter 3, data collection and management, which could be used to assess starting points and track progress toward goals, is highly variable across states and localities. Training and technical assistance providers will need to fully comprehend the nuances of the individual jurisdictions they will support. (See Chapter 3 for additional discussion on the expertise needed from training and technical assistance providers.) Assistance plans developed by the jurisdictions and their training and technical assistance providers should address data collection and reporting systems as a threshold activity, require outcome measures to establish baselines and track progress, and support multiyear commitments where needed.

A useful strategy observed in recent reform efforts is to bring stakeholders together to create a shared vision of reforms relevant to their work and to understand how their pieces of the system interact with others (National Research Council, 2013). Key partners typically include the police, intake staff, prosecutors, public defenders, judges, probation staff, citizens, and system-involved families (see also Box 2-1). Training and technical assistance providers must be able to engage each partner with information that is relevant to the interests and needs of those stakeholders. The training information needs to be tailored to the specific decisions that each partner makes. Data that could measure the effect of changes on the behaviors of these stakeholders should be collected and reported. If systematically analyzed and reported, this method of training and technical assistance could create enhanced and replicable models of practice.

Recommendation 4-2: OJJDP should develop a portfolio of training and technical assistance, properly balanced to be both strategic and tactical, to support the implementation of a developmental approach to juvenile justice reform. OJJDP should coordinate with agencies and organizations proficient in providing training and technical assistance based on the hallmarks of a developmental approach to juvenile justice reform. This proficiency should include historical experience working in system improvement efforts.

Recommendation 4-3: All applicants for technical assistance or demonstration grants sponsored by OJJDP should be required to show how they would use the assistance, either strategically or tactically, to implement or strengthen a developmental approach to juvenile justice reform.

THE CHALLENGE OF REDUCING RACIAL AND ETHNIC DISPARITIES IN THE JUVENILE JUSTICE SYSTEM

Reducing racial disparities and disproportionate representation is a critical element of juvenile justice reform.[7] Whatever their underlying causes, continued disparities call into question the fairness of the juvenile justice system and reinforce social disaffection and disrespect for the law among minority youths at a time when they are particularly sensitive to perceived discrimination and injustice (National Research Council, 2013, p. 194).

The literature reflects continuing uncertainty about the relative contribution of differential offending, differential enforcement and processing, and structural inequalities to these disparities. However, the current body of research suggests that poverty, social disadvantage, neighborhood disorganization, constricted opportunities, and other structural inequalities—which are strongly correlated with race/ethnicity—contribute to both differential offending and differential selection, especially at the front end of juvenile justice decision making. Because bias (whether conscious

---

[7]As the term has been used in the field, disproportionality represents a finding, based on a simple quantitative calculation, that the percentage of minority youths in the system at any stage is far greater than the percentage of minority youths in the general population would predict. Racial disparities are "between group differences" of *similarly situated* minority and majority youths, which "may stem from differences in offending, from laws or policies that differentially impact minority youth, or from racism in the juvenile justice system" (National Research Council, 2013, p. 214). Because disparities create disproportionality, disproportionality can be reduced indirectly through the elimination of disparities. (Piquero, 2008).

or unconscious) also plays a role, albeit of unknown magnitude, juvenile justice officials should embrace activities designed to increase awareness of these unconscious biases and to counteract them, as well as to detect and respond effectively to overt instances of discrimination. Although the juvenile justice system itself cannot alter the underlying structural causes of racial/ethnic disparities in juvenile justice, many conventional practices in enforcement and administration magnify these underlying disparities, and these contributors *are* within the reach of justice system policy makers.

(National Research Council, 2013, p. 239)

Congress first focused on racial disparities in the juvenile justice system in 1988 when it amended the JJDPA to require states that receive federal formula funds to ascertain the disproportionality in their systems. Subsequent actions included a refocus on disproportionate minority contact in 1992 and establishment of the disproportionality-ascertainment requirement as a core protection of the JJDPA Formula Grants Program in 2002. If the percentage of minority youths detained in secure detention facilities, secure correctional facilities, and lockups was disproportionate to their proportion in the general population, states were required to develop and implement plans for reducing the disparities. In order to determine the extent to which disproportionality exists in the jurisdictions, OJJDP requires states and localities to annually submit data known as the Relative Rate Index (RRI). The RRI measures the rates of differences between races at each decision point throughout the system. Specifically, it consists of three components: (1) a system map describing points of contact a juvenile may have with the system, (2) a method for calculating rates of activity by race/ethnicity at each point, and (3) a method to compare the rates of contact for different demographic groups at each of those stages (Feyerherm, 2011; Feyerherm et al., 2009; National Research Council, 2013). Although using the RRI allows one to ascertain patterns among groups and compare them across groups, the data are notably limited. The 2013 NRC report detailed these limitations and most critically noted:

An additional problem with the RRI calculations is that they do not come with any sort of statistical significance measure; thus, there is no way to measure whether an RRI of 1.0 is statistically significant—much less whether an RRI of 1.38 is significantly different from an RRI of 2.53. As a result, these sorts of official statistics provide limited leverage on the larger question of disproportionate minority youth contact with the juvenile justice system.

(National Research Council, 2013, pp. 217-219)

Because OJJDP's disparities reduction model only requires identification, assessment, program implementation, evaluation, and monitoring of disparities—that is, it does not actually require states to reduce disparities—very few, if any, states find themselves out of compliance with the core requirement of the JJDPA. [8] According to the W. Hayward Burns Institute, 61,000 youths were arrested in 2011, of which 75 percent were for nonviolent offenses. Of those incarcerated for nonviolent offenses, 65 percent were youths of color, making black youths 4.6 times more likely, Native American youths 3.2 times more likely, and Hispanic youths 1.8 times more likely than white youths to be incarcerated (W. Hayward Burns Institute for Juvenile Justice Fairness & Equity, 2013).[9] Data compiled from select counties exhibiting large declines in incarceration show that, even as reliance on confinement has decreased, youths of color represent a higher proportion of adjudicated youths in 2012 compared to 2002. In 2002, youths of color represented 67 percent of all dispositions (parole, placement, or secure confinement); in 2012, this rose to 80 percent of all dispositions. Similarly, 12 percent of the 2002 dispositions were for the secure confinement of youths of color (3 percent for white youths), whereas in 2012 the fraction who were youths of color increased to 22 percent of the dispositions for secure confinement, versus 6 percent for white youths (Davis et al., 2014).

These data indicate that, in spite of overwhelming compliance by the states with federal requirements, racial and ethnic disparities persist throughout the juvenile justice system. Notwithstanding a research and policy focus on this matter for more than two decades, remarkably little progress has been made. As a result, OJJDP has little empirical, evidence-based guidance to disseminate to the field. The 2013 NRC report noted that the lack of progress in this area was due, in part, to a lack of motivation; insufficient cross-system collaboration; inadequate resources;

---

[8]See http://www.ojjdp.gov/compliance/compliancedata.html [August 2014].

[9]For additional information, see *Mapping the Youth Incarceration Problem*. W. Haywood Burns Institute for Juvenile Justice Fairness & Equity, April 16, 2014. Available: http://www.burnsinstitute.org/blog/our-new-data-map-is-live/ [May 2014].

the extreme difficulties of disentangling the many complex, multilevel, and interrelated contributing factors; and deeply rooted structural biases (National Research Council, 2013, p. 213).

While too few examples of exemplary practice exist in this area, and the practices that do exist have been insufficiently researched, the committee notes that OJJDP's efforts have increased states' willingness to reduce disparities and create an infrastructure for monitoring and addressing them (National Research Council, 2013, p. 298). Reforms in the jurisdictions at the school/pre-arrest and detention stages offer an opportunity to examine how new approaches could help both to reduce disparities and to increase procedural justice.

Schools/Pre-arrest

There is increasing evidence that, even when other factors are held constant, every school suspension makes the next suspension, expulsion, drop-out, and arrest more likely. Successfully navigating school is a key developmental milestone for adolescents, and disruption to that path is not only harmful to proper adolescent development but may contribute to contact with the juvenile justice system. Research points to unwarranted disparities in suspensions—which lead to arrest, entrance into the juvenile justice system, and disruption from continued schooling—as a cause of disproportionality within the juvenile justice system (Fabelo et al., 2011; Morgan et al., 2014; New York Civil Liberties Union, 2013). Racial disparities continue to persist in out-of-school suspensions and expulsions, and studies show minority students and students with special education designations are suspended at rates disproportionate to their representation in the student body, especially for less serious misbehavior over which educators and law enforcement may exercise more discretion (Fabelo et al., 2011; U.S. Department of Education, 2014). An important vehicle for reducing referrals to juvenile court and reducing disparities in those referrals would be to reduce school-based arrests, particularly for trivial and normative school misconduct. While reforms like these apply to all students regardless of race, they have especially benefited youths of color who were disproportionately being suspended and arrested for lower severity misbehavior. Examples that warrant further study and possible replication include the following:

- **School-Based Diversion Initiative in Connecticut.** Launched in 2009, schools in Bridgeport and Hartford implemented strategies to reduce suspensions, expulsion, and arrests, including training for police on local diversion programs and empowering a review board to review misdemeanor arrests for possible diversion. In Hartford, arrests decreased by 78 percent from March through June 2012 compared to the previous year, contributing to a 28 percent decline in overall delinquency referrals to juvenile court from January to June 2012. Over the same period, Bridgeport schools saw a 40 percent decrease in school-based referrals. (Center for Children's Advocacy, 2013a; Morgan et al., 2014). In the 2012-2013 school year, Hartford experienced a 57 percent reduction in school-based arrests of youths of color and Bridgeport experienced a 34 percent reduction (Center for Children's Advocacy, 2013b).
- **Clayton County, Georgia.** Schools, police, and the juvenile court have agreed to a series of intermediate steps aimed at limiting the overall number of school referrals to the juvenile court and reducing the disproportionate contact of minorities with the juvenile justice system. The initiative has resulted in an 86 percent decrease in referrals for fighting and a 64 percent decrease in disruption-of-public-school offenses, especially for African American youths (Advancement Project, 2014; Morgan et al., 2014).

Building upon OJDDP's existing efforts, such as the Supportive School Discipline Initiative jointly announced by the secretary of education and the attorney general in July 2011, the agency is well positioned to help coordinate needed conversations and collaborations across youth-serving systems that include, but are not limited to, courts, schools, and law enforcement.

Detention

The 2013 NRC report detailed the historical context for the increasingly punitive approach to addressing delinquent behavior that resulted in greater reliance on detaining youths in secure facilities (National Research

Council, 2013, p. 32). In the past decade there has been a move away from restrictive correctional placements as a routine response, based on an emerging understanding of adolescent development and adolescent brain research and the implications for the justice system. In fact, this well-documented body of research led the 2013 NRC report to conclude that:

> There is no convincing evidence, [however], that confinement[10] of juvenile offenders beyond the minimum amount required to provide [intensive services], either in adult prisons or juvenile correctional institutions, appreciably reduces the likelihood of subsequent offending.
>
> (National Research Council, 2013, p. 181)

The effects of punitive policies disproportionately impacted minority youths, who experienced higher rates of arrest and detention than nonminority youths. This, coupled with the research demonstrating that confinement does not reduce the likelihood of re-offending, led many jurisdictions to undertake efforts both to reform the juvenile justice system and reduce racial disparities. Studies of these efforts, including an analysis of sites in the Juvenile Detention Alternatives Initiative, demonstrated that even a successful strategy for reducing detention would not necessarily result in a reduction in disparate outcomes (Annie E. Casey Foundation, 2013; Hinton Hoytt et al., 2001). Rather, the research suggests that a purposeful analysis of every decision point to examine the potential for contributing to the differences or inequities is needed to reduce racial disparities (W. Haywood Burns Institute for Juvenile Justice Fairness & Equity, 2013). The following examples of examining decision making at the point of detention demonstrate how such an analysis can lead to changes in practices that contributed to disproportionality and disparities:

- System stakeholders reviewed and revised their risk assessment instrument to ensure that there were no factors that increased the likelihood that minority youths would be detained while adding no value to the assessment of whether a youth was a risk of flight or re-arrest.
- Culturally relevant detention alternatives were created in neighborhoods with high minority populations where most arrests were made.
- Social workers were placed in the public defender's office to provide relevant information and alternative proposals to the courts for indigent youths at detention hearings.
- Case expediters were hired by the juvenile justice agency to constantly monitor whether youths were languishing unnecessarily in detention.

(Hinton Hoytt et al., 2001)

As with school-based approaches, these reforms—a better risk assessment instrument, improved access to detention alternatives, and an expedited system of processing cases—were available to all youths in the system and disproportionately benefited minority youths (Hinton Hoytt et al., 2001).

A New Approach to Addressing Racial and Ethnic Disparities

OJJDP has both the authority and the opportunity to work with the SAGs and the research community to develop a new approach requiring states to: (1) identify key decision points in their juvenile justice systems; (2) create data collection systems for each of those decision points disaggregated by race, ethnicity, and gender; (3) develop plans for reducing disparities at the decision points where disparities are apparent; (4) evaluate the outcomes of those plans; and (5) report those outcomes to OJJDP for monitoring purposes. This new approach also ought to coincide with phasing out use of the RRI in favor of new measures developed collaboratively through the process described above. The textured analysis of causes and solutions to disparities at each processing deci-

---

[10]While the discussion in this section is focused on youth in detention, which is defined as a short-term placement, the findings about confinement from the 2013 NRC report are relevant and important given that in 2011 (the most recent year for which data are available) more than 30 percent of youths were detained for more than 3 months and 5 percent were detained for 6 months to 2 years or more (Sickmund et al., 2013).

sion point will obviate the need for the RRI, which the 2013 NRC report, as noted above, critiqued as ineffectual (National Research Council, 2013, pp. 217-219). As that report found,

> [A]ny reform strategy should focus on eliminating formal and informal agency policies and practices that are shown to disproportionately disadvantage minority youth. To do so will require the identification of key decision points and decision-making criteria that appear in practice to fall disproportionately on minority youth and perhaps to reflect implicit bias.
>
> (National Research Council 2013, p. 240)

OJJDP can help promote a fairer and more equitable system, and therefore a more developmentally appropriate system, by (1) providing meaningful and well-informed training and technical assistance to the field, (2) supporting and highlighting best practices in reducing disparities, and (3) ensuring that learning networks are established among the demonstration sites to share knowledge in this important area.

- **Training and Technical Assistance.** Changing the differences in outcomes or rates of involvement at different points in the system by similarly situated minority and majority youths will require interventions targeting the specific factors leading to the differences. Training and technical assistance can help jurisdictions build the capacity to conduct a critical analysis of the specific conditions in their communities before initiating interventions.
- **Supporting Best Practices.** OJJDP can partner with state and local governments to support the analysis of disparities at different decision points and the identification of the factors leading to disparities, such as unequal access to opportunity and resources, limited access to services, lack of community resources, social problems, individual bias, and institutional racism. While the juvenile justice system itself cannot alter the underlying structural factors that cause racial and ethnic disparities, it can work as part of a larger collaborative effort and it can work to reform its own practices that magnify disparities. OJJDP can assist by supporting rigorous evaluations and developing the scientific evidence regarding the impact of interventions on the contributing factors.
- **Learning Networks.** As part of the Demonstration Grant Program described more fully below,[11] OJJDP can partner with jurisdictions to identify, implement, document, and share reform strategies that ameliorate the effects of disadvantage and discrimination by reducing unnecessary system referral, involvement, and confinement. The demonstration grant program should include strategic, in-depth technical assistance to jurisdictions and the development of "learning networks." The jurisdictions competitively selected should include those that consist of populations with high proportions of minorities, so that any effects on disparities can have the largest impacts and the jurisdictions can serve as national models to grow and implement successful policies nationwide. These promising approaches can be highlighted by OJJDP, disseminated to the field, and supported through partnerships with appropriate federal and national-organization partners.

The committee believes that these strategies will position OJJDP to assist states with the four reform strategies specified in the 2013 NRC report for moving forward toward the goal of reducing racial disparities: paying special attention to the arrest and detention stages at the front end of the system, reviewing school disciplinary practices and eliminating those that are punitive and discretionary and likely to result in a referral to the juvenile justice system, eliminating formal and informal agency policies and practices that are shown to disproportionately disadvantage minority youths, and increasing the accountability of governments for reducing racial and ethnic disparities.

Recommendation 4-4: OJJDP should establish new approaches for identifying racial and ethnic disparities across the juvenile justice system, promulgate new guidelines for reducing and eliminating racial and ethnic

---

[11]Relying on a system reform and developmental framework to improve safety, fairness, and youth outcomes, the multisite demonstration project described below would require data-driven planning; evidence-based and research-informed best practices in policy, practice, and programming; state re-investment commitments; and independent evaluation to create practical, replicable, and sustainable examples of comprehensive change.

disparities, build the internal capacity and/or establish partnerships for assisting states with these new requirements, and strengthen the role of State Advisory Groups (SAGs) in monitoring the new guidelines by providing training and technical assistance to SAGs.

DEMONSTRATION GRANTS

As noted in Chapter 3, OJJDP could help guide the juvenile justice field by leveraging its available funding and establishing creative partnerships with experienced agencies to develop and offer demonstration programs. A multiyear pilot program or demonstration program could be developed to support, with funding and technical assistance, jurisdictions demonstrating a readiness to implement change and create a developmentally appropriate system. Each demonstration or pilot jurisdiction could be required to formulate a comprehensive reform plan designed to promote accountability, ensure fairness, and reduce the risk of further delinquency in ways compatible with the hallmarks of a developmental approach.

To be selected, jurisdictions could be required to demonstrate a willingness to collect and analyze data to measure youth outcomes and system improvement progress over time; foster partnerships that reach across traditional program categories such as health, behavioral health, social services, education, juvenile justice, housing, and workforce development; and identify avenues for meaningful youth and family participation in the design and execution of the jurisdiction's plan.

The outcomes of these projects should provide replicable guidance for state and local jurisdictions across the country. These sites ought to be viewed from the outset as "learning laboratories." Since this is an area without proven, independently researched models, evaluators will need to engage in "action research" in an iterative process analogous to open trials in the medical arena. During the demonstration phase, evaluators, technical assistance providers, OJJDP personnel and officials, and SAG members in states with demonstration sites will need to periodically convene to share lessons and create a learning community.

Recommendation 4-5: In partnership with other federal agencies and the philanthropic community, OJJDP should develop a multiyear demonstration project designed to provide substantial technical assistance and financial support to selected states and localities to develop a comprehensive plan for reforming the state's juvenile justice system based on a developmental approach. The demonstration grant should include a requirement for strategies that reduce racial and ethnic disparities and the unnecessary use of confinement as well as other hallmarks of a developmental approach. OJJDP should ensure that State Advisory Group (SAG) members in states with demonstration sites are intimately involved in their state's pilot projects and help disseminate lessons learned to other states' SAGs.

REALIGNMENT AND REINVESTMENT STRATEGIES

In the justice field, recent reforms have attempted to balance developmentally appropriate policy choices and budgets while still protecting public safety. In cash-strapped times, some states and counties have found that through realignment, reinvestment strategies, or a combination of both, they are able to reduce institutional commitments and capture the savings to fund community programs for youths who would have been committed to placement otherwise (National Research Council, 2013, p. 272). Realignment is a process of organizational and structural modifications: "[r]econfiguring the justice system to expand the roles and responsibilities of local government while reducing or even eliminating the direct control of state government" (Butts and Evans, 2011, p. 12). Reinvestment is the creation of financial incentives to change system practices, such as diverting funds that would otherwise be used for confinement to evidence-based alternatives. RECLAIM Ohio and Redeploy Illinois relied upon reinvestment reform strategies; Wayne County, Michigan, and New York City used a realignment model to facilitate change; and California and Texas used a hybrid of both strategies (Butts and Evans, 2011). Although research on realignment and reinvestment strategies is not extensive, it appears that the primary goals of such strategies—reducing institutional populations, redirecting funds to community-based programs, and reducing recidivism—are being achieved (Butts and Evans, 2011).

Current examples of realignment/reinvestment systems reform approaches—including those from criminal justice and mental health—offer a number of important lessons. In almost every case, it is apparent that reform and organizational change take time and energy; they require building relationships and trust and the continuing engagement and education of stakeholders and decision makers. Additionally, documented assurance and measured outcomes that ensure that resources will be reinvested in the intended manner seem to be critical for successful reform. For example, legislatures of some states in the Bureau of Justice Assistance's Justice Reinvestment Initiative program did not mandate reinvestment of criminal justice spending due to budgetary or political concerns. As a result, cost savings from the program were not reinvested in community-based justice programs and interventions (Austin et al., 2013; LaVigne et al., 2014). Reform can also be hampered by staff and policy-maker turnover, lack of public support, and high-profile incidents that undermine the goals of reform (LaVigne et al., 2014). Political compromises can water down reforms and hamper their implementation (Austin et al., 2013).

In the mental health field, evaluations of reforms have shown tempered success. Goldman and colleagues (2000) concluded that since experimental studies have not detected positive clinical outcomes in the presence of continuity-of-care initiatives, reorganization of service systems may increase organizational cooperation but may be only as effective as the clinical services, programs, and practices instituted as part of the reform. Scheffler and colleagues (2001) found that the effects of realignment in California's mental health system were not consistent across the state, which they thought was likely due to socioeconomic and political difference among local mental health authorities, prompting them to conclude that economic differences among regions can affect the success and equity of realignment programs. In the juvenile justice field, an early evaluation of California's recent judicial realignment noted similar concerns regarding the availability of programs throughout the state, as some counties are at the forefront of instituting reforms while others, for historical or cultural reasons, lag behind (Rappaport, 2013).

Given these early findings, the committee thinks that the success of realignment and reinvestment will probably rest on the uniform development of community alternative services. OJJDP can play a role in the juvenile justice field by guiding the development and incorporation of alternatives to confinement. OJJDP can also advance the state of knowledge on these strategies by inviting competitive proposals for conducting further research into realignment and reinvestment approaches. OJJDP can assess and evaluate the implementation of these strategies and assemble lessons learned. This evaluation would include focusing on system reform outcomes, incentives for changing practices, and consolidation of the data efforts. In addition, OJJDP could provide assistance to states engaged in or seeking to use these strategies, to ensure that they are implementing a developmental approach to their reform and decision making.

5

Partnerships

Before youths become justice involved,[1] they are members of families and communities and may receive services from community-based agencies, schools, and other government-funded agencies, such as those charged with child protection and those providing health and mental health services. As they come into contact with the justice system in their neighborhoods and communities, they will come in contact with law enforcement, courts, diversion programs, judges, attorneys (defense and prosecution), probation, detention, corrections, and social service providers. The potential partners in a local juvenile justice system are endless; the degree to which they will develop as partners is unique to each jurisdiction and to the strengths of the partnering organizations and individuals. Each of these partners must be committed to a common goal, such as the one envisioned here of a developmental approach to juvenile justice reform, to realize the desired outcomes in each state, local, and tribal jurisdiction.

The Office of Juvenile Justice and Delinquency Prevention (OJJDP) is identified as the federal agency specifically authorized to prevent and control juvenile delinquency and improve the juvenile justice system. As such, it is the federal agency that interacts with state and local courts and human service agencies, regulatory bodies, and funding sources that in turn interact with all the potential partners in a local juvenile justice system. It is also the agency that has the greatest opportunity to facilitate not only individual partnerships but also a high-impact collective initiative in juvenile justice reform.

Kania and Kramer (2011, p. 39) contrasted what they called "technical" and "adaptive" problems in their review of large-scale social change. Their comparison described "technical" problems as well-defined with solutions within the ability of one or a few organizations and adaptive problems as "complex, the answer is not known, and even if it were, no single entity has the resources or authority to bring about the necessary change." Juvenile justice reform is a response to this second type of problem.

As a federal agency for a system that is governed by states and localities, OJJDP can assume several roles: leader, funder, facilitator, supporter, and backbone organization for juvenile justice reform. Often it serves these roles in collaboration with other agencies. OJJDP reported to the committee that it is currently participating in 30 federal interagency initiatives, which are listed in Box 5-1, many within the U.S. Department of Justice (DOJ) and some representing multiple federal departments.

The primary outcome reported for these efforts was to increase communication, collaboration, and informa-

---

[1] See Terminology section in Chapter 1 for definitions of "system-involved youths" and other terms introduced by the committee for this report.

BOX 5-1
OJJDP Participation in Federal Interagency Initiatives

Attorney General's Task Force on American Indian/Alaska Native Children Exposed to Violence
Coordinating Council on Juvenile Justice and Delinquency Prevention
Data and Research Committee of the Senior Policy Operation Group on Human Trafficking
Defending Childhood Initiative
DOJ Indigent Defense Work Group
    Enhancing Youth Access to Justice Subcommittee of Indigent Defense Work Group
Evidence-Based Policy Research Work Group
FBI/ICAC Work Group
Federal Interagency Forum on Child and Family Statistics
Federal Interagency ReEntry Council
    Subgroup on Juvenile ReEntry and Transitions
    Subgroup on ReEntry Research Network
    Subgroup on Children of Incarcerated Parents
Federal Partners for Suicide Prevention
Federal Partners in Bullying Prevention Steering Committee
Federal Working Group on the National Strategy on the Prevention of Child Exploitation
Forum on Youth Violence Prevention
Indian Alcohol and Substance Abuse Committee
Interagency Coordinating Council on Fetal Alcohol Spectrum Disorders
Interagency Coordinating Council on Fetal Alcohol Spectrum Disorders—Justice Issues Work Group
Interagency Task Force on Missing and Exploited Children
Interagency Work Group on Youth Programs
National Coordinating Committee on School Health and Safety
OJP Institutional Review Board
OJP Juvenile Justice Research Group
OJP Tiered Evidence Work Group
OJP Wide TTA Managers Meeting
Supportive School Discipline Leadership Collaborative
Victim Services Committee of the Senior Policy Operating Group on Human Trafficking
Work Group on Human Trafficking

NOTE: DOJ = U.S. Department of Justice; FBI/ICAC = Federal Bureau of Investigation/Internet Crimes Against Children Task Force; OJP = Office of Justice Programs; TTA = Training and Technical Assistance.
SOURCE: OJJDP presentation to the Committee on a Prioritized Plan to Implement a Developmental Approach in Juvenile Justice Reform, January 21-22, 2014.

---

tion-sharing. In the absence of any performance measures to indicate how progress toward the stated outcome is determined, it is not clear how OJJDP leverages these work groups to advance its overarching agenda, nor is it clear how the work group activities are integrated with other OJJDP activities, including several of the seven interagency work groups for which it is the lead agency. This lack of clear measures of success may explain why some stakeholders express concern that OJJDP is spread too thin and that this diminishes its ability to lead a national juvenile justice reform agenda. The committee believes OJJDP should be judicious in its involvement with these work groups, focusing its efforts as an agency and those of individual staff on those work groups that have a clearly articulated role in an agenda for juvenile justice reform, and limit the amount of time spent on information-sharing where there is no action plan.

The U.S. Government Accountability Office (2005, p. 2) has identified collaboration as "any joint activity that is intended to produce more public value than could be produced when the organizations act alone." This should be the intended outcome for every partnership that OJJDP may enter into to achieve its mission. While it is the only federal agency specifically authorized to prevent and control juvenile delinquency and improve the juvenile justice system, it is not the only agency that has an opportunity to contribute to this mission.

A 2012 report from the U.S. Government Accountability Office (GAO) outlined some common barriers to effective collaboration that may, and likely do, represent challenges to OJJDP's efforts to collaborate. These challenges include the desire of an organization to maintain control (i.e., turf protection); conflicting service priorities and rules; different missions, goals, and standards for achievement; a lack of mutual respect, understanding, and trust; reluctance to share information or constraints on doing so; incompatible professional cultures; different information technology systems; and lack of understanding of a partner's limitations (Harbert et al., 1997; Patti et al., 2003). The literature suggests methods OJJDP can utilize to overcome these common barriers and help alleviate organizational and cultural gaps between partners; for example, establishing networks among the administrative staff of participating agencies, co-locating, providing well-focused training, creating common terminologies, and fostering open communication (Bardach, 1998; U.S. Government Accountability Office, 2012).

Other factors that the GAO has identified as enhancing and sustaining collaborative efforts involve engagement in eight specific practices: "defining and articulating a common outcome; establishing mutually reinforcing or joint strategies; identifying and addressing needs by leveraging resources; agreeing on roles and responsibilities; establishing compatible policies, procedures, and other means to operate across agency boundaries; developing mechanisms to monitor, evaluate, and report on results of collaborative efforts; reinforcing agency accountability for collaborative efforts through agency plans and reports; and reinforcing individual accountability for collaborative efforts through performance management systems" (U.S. Government Accountability Office, 2005, pp. 14-15). The committee notes that in addition to the strategies outlined in this chapter, there are resources available to OJJDP as it addresses the factors and conditions that must be present at both the federal and state/local/tribal level to successfully confront a complex social problem, such as juvenile delinquency and juvenile justice system improvement.[2] OJJDP has the opportunity to redefine its role in all of its partnerships in ways that will advance a developmentally appropriate juvenile justice system. In this chapter, the committee identifies opportunities for OJJDP to reshape current collaborations and to establish important new partnerships.

U.S. DEPARTMENT OF JUSTICE

A key opportunity for strategic partnerships at the federal level is within DOJ itself. While OJJDP is the federal agency tasked to improve the juvenile justice system, it is one of five agencies within the Office of Justice Programs (OJP) and one of many other agencies within DOJ. Implementation of a developmental approach to juvenile justice will require OJP and DOJ's support and leadership. The committee recognizes that acceptance of the hallmarks of a developmental approach to juvenile justice reform across all DOJ agencies is a necessary condition for carrying out the strategy outlined in this report.

Where there is a common agenda across DOJ agencies, such as in responding to children exposed to violence,[3] multiple agencies engage in mutually reinforcing activities and leverage their resources so that collectively they have a greater impact than individual projects or single-agency funding to address complex problems. However, a shared agenda should not divert any partnering agency from its primary mission; each agency should be able to advance its particular mission in the context of the overall collaboration. DOJ and OJP play an important role in ensuring that agencies within the department are able to collaborate without compromising the focus on their core mission. For example, it would be prudent for OJJDP's efforts to focus largely on justice-involved youths while it engages the broader agenda of prevention with other DOJ offices and other federal partners (such as those within

---

[2]For example, federal and state agencies have utilized Results-Based Accountability to guide collaborative efforts and the Results Score Card to measure outcomes. See http://resultsleadership.org/ http://resultsaccountability.com/.

[3]The Defending Childhood Initiative, based on the report from the Task Force on Children Exposed to Violence, "leverages existing resources across DOJ to focus on preventing, addressing, reducing, and more fully understanding childhood exposure to violence." The report is available: http://www.justice.gov/defendingchildhood/about-initiative.html [May 2014].

the Department of Health and Human Services) that have primary prevention as a central mission.[4] It is critical for OJJDP to maintain a steadfast focus on the populations within its mission, even while leading or participating in efforts with a scope broader than justice-involved youths.

In the area of youth violence, agencies within DOJ and other federal agencies are working on joint programs such as Second Chance (Re-entry), Children of Incarcerated Parents, and My Brother's Keeper. These efforts provide an opportunity for OJJDP, as a key agency within DOJ, to voice an agenda on the reform of the juvenile justice system as part of a larger community-oriented policy commitment focused on youth violence and delinquency prevention.

A significant example of nesting OJJDP's agenda in a broader DOJ initiative is evident in the opportunities to collaborate with the Office of Community Oriented Policing Services (COPS). The law enforcement community is key in reforming the juvenile justice system, and COPS is a critical partner for OJJDP to reach that community. There are opportunities to embed the hallmarks of a developmental approach in existing COPS-OJJDP activities, as well as to create new joint initiatives.

OJP has made a strong commitment to strategic alignment and partnership.[5] OJP includes OJJDP, the Bureau of Justice Assistance (BJA), the Bureau of Justice Statistics, National Institute of Justice, and Office for Victims of Crimes. Currently OJJDP has, or could have, a major role in several initiatives that present an opportunity for implementing the recommendations of the 2013 National Research Council (NRC) report and for incorporating developmentally based principles of juvenile justice reform in the work of all OJP programs. As previously noted, initiatives such as the Second Chance (Re-entry), Children of Incarcerated Parents, and My Brother's Keeper are all joint OJP department activities and present opportunities to connect different parts of the justice system to the hallmarks of a developmental approach by utilizing the BJA model of demonstration projects and to creatively finance such projects within existing or augmented appropriations.

Recommendation 5-1: The U.S. Department of Justice, including but not limited to the Office of Justice Programs, should authorize, publicly support, and actively partner with OJJDP to provide federal support for developmentally oriented juvenile justice reform in states, localities, and tribal jurisdictions. The federal initiative should include strategic training and technical assistance; demonstration programs; and a range of incentives to states, localities, and tribes to achieve specific outcomes for justice-involved youths, as well as specific system changes.

FEDERAL PARTNERSHIPS

In an environment of unlimited time and financial and staff resources, OJJDP might be able to pursue every partnership possibility at the federal level. However, when there are limited staff and financial resources, as well as limited time, the committee believes OJJDP should focus activities and partnerships on those opportunities that will have the greatest impact on the goal of a more developmentally appropriate juvenile justice system. OJJDP should focus on developing and supporting partnerships that will help the agency develop and implement a learning curriculum for staff (see Chapter 3) and design a demonstration grant program (see Chapter 4) by, for example, borrowing experts in national organizations and foundations and engaging families of justice-involved youths. In addition, OJJDP should identify opportunities for strategic collaborations that address the hallmarks of a developmental approach (see Chapter 2).

For example, to support the goal of a fair and accountable system, OJJDP could explore developing practice guidelines for pre-petition diversion with the Department of Education and COPS. Or it could establish as a coordinating council priority increasing youth and family participation as full partners in system improvement and intensifying family engagement in juvenile justice proceedings.

---

[4]For example, to the extent that OJJDP is carrying out responsibilities assigned under the Missing Children's Assistance Act or the Victims of Child Abuse Act, the committee believes that appropriations under those statutes need be adequate to support OJJDP's assigned activities so that they do not divert agency resources from its mission under the JJDPA.

[5]Remarks of the Honorable Karol V. Mason, Assistant Attorney General, Office of Justice Programs, at the meeting of the Committee on a Prioritized Plan to Implement a Developmental Approach in Juvenile Justice Reform, February 14, 2014, Washington, DC.

A third example involves strengthening the existing partnership with the Substance Abuse and Mental Health Services Administration (SAMHSA),which presents an opportunity to incorporate the lessons learned in mental health services regarding family engagement. SAMHSA's Systems of Care initiative has resulted in stronger family involvement and engagement in the delivery of mental health services at the local level. It has been extended to those families who are served through child welfare systems. In some local jurisdictions, there are also lessons learned for involving and engaging families of system-involved youths. These local lessons learned present opportunities for OJJDP to incorporate a developmental approach into Systems of Care and to import the developmentally appropriate family engagement strategies from that initiative into the reform of the juvenile justice system.

Recommendation 5-2: OJJDP should initiate and support collaborative partnerships at the federal, state, local, and tribal levels and should use them strategically to advance the goal of a developmentally appropriate juvenile justice system.

Role of the Coordinating Council on Juvenile Justice and Delinquency Prevention

The Juvenile Justice and Delinquency Prevention Act (JJDPA) of 1974, as amended, established the Coordinating Council on Juvenile Justice and Delinquency Prevention as an independent organization in the executive branch of the federal government. The coordinating council is composed of representatives from the statutory member agencies (the Departments of Justice, Housing and Urban Development, Labor, Education, and Health and Human Services; the Executive Office for National Drug Control Policy; the Corporation for National and Community Service; and the Immigration and Customs Enforcement Agency of the Department of Homeland Security), plus three members appointed by the Speaker of the House of Representatives, three appointed by the majority leader of the Senate, and three by the President. All appointed members are to be practitioners in the field of juvenile justice who are not officers or employees of the United States.

As discussed in Chapter 2, one hallmark for a developmental approach to juvenile justice reform is incorporating the perspective of system-involved youth and families in decision making around juvenile justice interventions and reform agendas for system improvements. The coordinating council, which includes juvenile justice stakeholders, provides an opportunity to fully engage justice-involved youths and families at the federal level and to include their perspectives in guiding policy, practice, and reform. As noted by Pennell and colleagues (2011, p. 11):

> . . . through the Second Chance Act of 2007 and the support of the Office of Juvenile Justice and Delinquency Prevention, reentry initiatives are cognizant of the need for family engagement and other ecological approaches. The Second Chance Act has underscored the role of family engagement in a youth's transition home from a juvenile justice facility and is funding family and community collaborative strategies.

The committee heard broad support from across the juvenile justice field for family engagement. In a presentation to the committee, a representative of the Campaign for Youth Justice noted the desire of juvenile justice system advocates to have family and youth voices included on the coordinating council.[6] In another presentation, OJJDP voiced recognition of the value of engaging youth and families at the local level.[7] At the most recent meeting of the coordinating council (April 2014), family and youth perspectives were included in the informal networking that took place after the meeting. In remarks to the committee, Assistant Attorney General Karol Mason indicated the possibility of family engagement through a seat on the coordinating council.[8]

---

[6]Presentation by Carmen Daugherty to the Committee on a Prioritized Plan to Implement a Developmental Approach in Juvenile Justice Reform, February 14, 2014.

[7]OJJDP Presentation to the Committee on a Prioritized Plan to Implement a Developmental Approach in Juvenile Justice Reform, January 21-22, 2014.

[8]Presentation to the Committee on a Prioritized Plan to Implement a Developmental Approach in Juvenile Justice Reform by Assistant Attorney General Karol Mason on February 14, 2014. See Appendix A for a list of speakers and interviews.

Recommendation 5-3: OJJDP should establish and convene, on an ongoing basis, a Family Advisory Group to the Coordinating Council on Juvenile Justice and Delinquency Prevention, composed of youths and families whose lives have been impacted by the juvenile justice system.

The purpose of the coordinating council is to coordinate relevant federal work and support state and local juvenile justice programs. The most recent charter for the coordinating council, which was approved in April 2012 for a 2-year period, states that:

> The function of the Council shall be to coordinate Federal juvenile delinquency programs (in cooperation with State and local juvenile justice programs), all Federal programs and activities that detain or care for unaccompanied juveniles, and all Federal programs relating to missing and exploited children. The Council shall examine how the separate programs can be coordinated among Federal, State, and local governments to better serve at-risk children and juveniles and shall make recommendations to the President, and to the Congress, at least annually with respect to the coordination of overall policy and development of objectives and priorities for all Federal juvenile delinquency programs and activities and all Federal programs and activities that detain or care for unaccompanied juveniles. . . . "[9]

Section 3 of the charter also outlines a scope of activities that includes (1) a review of programs and practices of federal agencies to determine whether they are consistent with the JJDPA, (2) the ability to make recommendations regarding joint funding proposals by OJJDP and council member agencies, (3) review of the reasons for federal agencies to take juveniles into custody, and (4) the ability to make recommendations on how to improve practices and facilities holding these identified juveniles.

In examining the work of the coordinating council, the committee received information from OJJDP staff, interviewed members of the council, and reviewed the council Website and materials. Acting on the charter described above, the council's recent accomplishments, as identified by OJJDP,[10] appear to be the exchange of information on critical initiatives and dissemination of information to a national audience. External stakeholders have an opportunity to observe coordinating council meetings in person or by webcast. The committee noted that while OJJDP staff report accomplishments that started with an exchange of information at a council meeting and then developed into follow-up work,[11] it was difficult to identify the strategic actions of the coordinating council. For example, OJJDP staff report that the 2013 NRC report now permeates the agency's work with federal partners. However, the committee was unable to discern whether and how OJJDP has used the authority of the coordinating council to reinforce the developmental approach in each of the council's member agencies or to recommend future federal activities. The committee did determine that several documents on the coordinating council website do not reflect a coordinated approach to delinquency prevention or juvenile justice and are significantly out of date.[12] For example, the fiscal year 2008 Delinquency Development Statements, while no longer required, were used for joint planning and appear to be the most recent expressions of the council's collective efforts. The statements are a useful listing of programs and grants but do not describe or demonstrate how these programs are designed to address a joint outcome or shared goal.

By working with its federal partners on the coordinating council, OJJDP has the opportunity to lead and coordinate collaborative program initiatives focused on the hallmarks of a developmental approach. A current model that may be useful for OJJDP to examine is the administration's Neighborhood Revitalization Initiative, which brings together the White House Domestic Policy Council; White House Office of Urban Affairs; and the Departments of Housing and Urban Development, Education, Justice, Health and Human Services, and Treasury

---

[9]Charter: Coordinating Council on Juvenile Justice and Delinquency Prevention, signed by the Attorney General, April 20, 2012, page 3. Available: http://www.juvenilecouncil.gov/materials/AG_approval_and_signed_Charter.pdf [May 2014].

[10]Personal communication from representatives of the OJJDP coordinating council staff, April 11, 2014.

[11]Personal communication from representatives of the OJJDP coordinating council staff, April 11, 2014.

[12]The coordinating council's Website contains the most recent plan "Combating Violence and Delinquency: The National Juvenile Justice Action Plan" from 1996. The most recent Federal Agencies Delinquency Development Statements demonstrating their collective contribution to reducing or preventing delinquency are from 2008, and the hyperlink to "A Shared Vision for Youth," the collaborative effort to address violence, is broken. The materials on individual agency Websites date from 2008. The Website is *Coordinating Council on Juvenile Justice and Delinquency Prevention,* http://www.juvenilecouncil.gov/index.html [May 2014].

"in support of local solutions to revitalize and transform neighborhoods. The interagency strategy is designed to catalyze and empower local action while busting silos, prioritizing public-private partnerships, and making existing programs more effective and efficient."[13] Together, these agencies and offices have integrated several related programs, targeted resources in a coordinated grant strategy, provided joint technical assistance, and shared best practices. This may be a prototype for work that OJJDP could lead through the coordinating council, which has greater statutory authority[14] and leadership involvement than the Neighborhood Revitalization Initiative and therefore has the potential to accomplish even more. OJJDP could also look to past coordinating council activities, such as SafeFutures, Safe Schools/Healthy Students, and Safe Kids/Safe Streets, for examples of shared outcomes, multiyear commitments of technical assistance and funding, and agency guidance that could be instructive as the council re-asserts its leadership capacity.

If the coordinating council is used strategically, it can serve an important role in addressing the barriers to collaboration outlined by the GAO (U.S. Government Accountability Office, 2012) by laying out an agenda for the federal partners that defines a common outcome; establishes mutually reinforcing or joint activities; addresses needs by leveraging resources; agrees on roles and responsibilities; establishes compatible policies, procedures, and other means to operate across agency boundaries; develops mechanisms to monitor, evaluate, and report on results; reinforces agency accountability for collaborative efforts through agency plans and reports; and reinforces individual accountability through performance management systems. All of this should be visible to all stakeholders. For example, OJJDP can work through the council to launch an interdepartmental effort to involve the relevant community agencies (e.g., police, probation, prosecutors, schools, health and human services) in establishing developmentally appropriate diversionary tools to reduce the number of youths coming into the system, with particular attention directed to the issue of school referrals to law enforcement that may be criminalizing normal adolescent misbehaviors.

Recommendation 5-4: OJJDP, with the support of the attorney general, should use the Coordinating Council on Juvenile Justice and Delinquency Prevention strategically to implement key components of developmentally oriented juvenile justice reform through interagency, intergovernmental (federal-state-local partnering), and public-private partnering activities with specific measurable objectives.

Federal Budget Opportunities

Federal funding to serve adolescents is typically categorical and focused on narrowly defined purposes or problems. States and localities desiring to tap federal funding for serving youths involved in the juvenile justice system must navigate a web of agency policies, funding restrictions, eligibility requirements, and other complexities. The result is a fragmented service delivery system that frequently fails to meet the multiple needs of system-involved youths (Hayes, 2002; Moore, 2012). Durable, long-term, systemic improvements that result in improved outcomes for youths in the juvenile justice system will require high-quality, coordinated services and opportunities in the community. States and local governments have demonstrated their ability to improve outcomes for children and youths when provided access to integrated funding (National Collaborative on Workforce and Disability for Youth, 2006; National Governors Association Center for Best Practices, 2004; Rust, 1999). If available federal grant programs are leveraged effectively, they can be used to create a service delivery continuum in communities reaching from primary prevention to aftercare, while supporting systems building, research, and data collection.

Given the sheer number of distinct federal programs relevant to the juvenile justice system and a developmentally informed approach to reforming it, the committee commissioned a paper by The Finance Project to catalog the relevant programs in seven domains: Health and Well-Being, Academic Success, Youth Development and Engagement, Supportive Families and Communities, Accountability and Fairness, Other Supportive Services,

---

[13]See *Neighborhood Revitalization Initiative* on the website of the White House Office of Urban Affairs: http://www.whitehouse.gov/administration/eop/oua/initiatives/neighborhood-revitalization [May 2014].

[14]As noted in the April 2012 charter, the Coordinating Council on Juvenile Justice and Delinquency Prevention was established by Section 206 of the JJDPA.

and System-Building and Support (Hayes, 2014). Table 5-1 summarizes that catalog, which is available online,[15] and its subcategories for activities in each domain. Funding sources for these subcategories were identified and reviewed, where applicable, by stages of youth involvement in the juvenile justice system: primary prevention, diversion, community supervision, placement, and aftercare. Approximately 110 federal programs were identified that support initiatives for youths who are involved in or at risk of involvement in the juvenile justice system. Programs related to the causes and consequences of juvenile delinquency are authorized under 11 different federal departments and agencies, of which OJJDP manages the smallest number of grant programs with the least amount of resources (Hayes, 2014). OJJDP is the only agency that would use its funds directly for juvenile justice system improvement. As discussed in Chapter 3, restoring OJJDP's funding and capacity and flexibility would advance the nation's reform movement. However, even in its current state, by working with its federal partners, OJJDP could use information in the catalog to inform its consideration of interagency initiatives and to provide guidance and support for states, localities, and other stakeholders on ways to leverage federal funding.

Even if leveraged and used creatively, federal funds will not provide support for all of the components of developmentally oriented juvenile justice reform. While federal funding currently supports an array of services, a significant number of the programs are focused on substance abuse and behavioral health services. Relatively few fund family support, family literacy, and other services to strengthen the capacity of parents and family members to address truancy, school dropout, and other adolescent risk-taking behaviors that lead to or are associated with juvenile justice involvement. In addition, only three programs fund indigent defense, and there is little to no funding for training of the judiciary or prosecutors, who are critical components of a fair and equitable system (Hayes, 2014). These are key elements of a developmentally informed juvenile justice system, and OJJDP will need to work with private foundations or encourage states to address these resource gaps as part of a reform effort.

A coordinated federal approach to funding provides each agency with the opportunity to leverage the collective impact of its resources and advance its agency-specific missions. In addition, availability of and access to flexible federal resources will encourage states and localities to engage in system reform efforts. The options for federal partners to provide these resources include all of the following:

- Use existing administrative authority to establish flexibility in current federal funding. For example, flexibility could be created through waivers of the state match, program eligibility requirements, or grant timelines.
- Dedicate a share of, or create a preference within, an existing federal program to specifically serve justice-involved youths. For example, housing incentives could be provided for youths returning to their communities from placement by prioritizing vouchers for this population.
- Commit discretionary funding, for example, to create flexible resources for use by jurisdictions participating in a demonstration program or to address resource gaps such as family support services or indigent defense.
- Create a pool of federal funding by bundling several programs under a single initiative. For example, separate categorical funding sources could be aligned and delivered through an OJJDP demonstration project.

Recommendation 5-5: OJJDP should work with its federal agency and Coordinating Council on Juvenile Justice and Delinquency Prevention partners (i) to blend or leverage available federal funds to support OJJDP demonstration projects and (ii) to provide guidance to eligible grantees on leveraging federal funding at the state or local level.

---

[15]The catalog contains a matrix of funding for activities in the seven domains, a one-page description for each funding program with the name of the program, authorizing legislation, brief description of the program's purpose, how funds may be used, the application requirements, and the process (Hayes, 2014). Available: http://sites.nationalacademies.org/dbasse/claj/dbasse_088937 [August 2014].

TABLE 5-1 Federal Funding for Youths with, or at Risk of, Juvenile Justice Involvement (ages 10-24 years)

Health and Well-being	Academic Success	Youth Development and Engagement	Supportive Families and Communities	Accountability and Fairness	Other Supportive Services	System-Building and Support
Prevention and treatment of fetal alcohol syndrome, child abuse or neglect, trauma	Academic support	Character building	Family support services	Law enforcement and policing practices (youth-related)	Professional development (for practitioners providing discipline/services to youths)	Professional development (for practitioners providing discipline/services to youths)
Medical and dental care	School discipline	Civic engagement	Family literacy	School resource officers	Housing	Case management
Nutrition	Other: arts/culture; family literacy; ESL*	Community service	Family counseling	Teen courts/specialty courts	Transportation	Planning coordination and collaboration
Substance abuse treatment	Bullying prevention	Mentoring	Peer interventions	Indigent defense	Collaborations—community agencies	Evaluation
Mental health and behavioral services (including anger management)	Dropout prevention and recovery	Vocational and occupational training; work experience	Violence reduction	Risk assessment	Short-term crisis placements	Technical assistance and training
Recreation and fitness	Alternative schooling, GED*	Job placement	Gang awareness and diversion	Day or evening reporting centers	Alternatives to detention	Data and information technology
Reproductive services	Special education supports; transition planning	Summer employment	Financial literacy		Multisystem service centers	Facilities improvement; management systems improvement

*ESL = English as a Second Language; GED = General Educational Development [tests].
SOURCE: Hayes (2014).

NATIONAL ORGANIZATION PARTNERSHIPS

Collaboration with national organization partners also will be critical to achieving the goal of a developmentally appropriate juvenile justice system. OJJDP has successfully adopted the dual role of leadership and partnership in the past with practitioners, affiliated youths serving partner agencies, and organizations to support decision makers in the juvenile justice arena (see also Box 2-2).

The Federal Advisory Committee on Juvenile Justice and the Coalition for Juvenile Justice

Two national organizations that can facilitate a strong partnership between OJJDP and the states are the Federal Advisory Committee on Juvenile Justice (FACJJ) and the Coalition for Juvenile Justice (CJJ). The FACJJ comprises representatives from a number of State Advisory Groups. The CJJ includes the State Advisory Groups plus individuals and other organizations, all focused on juvenile justice. OJJDP would be well served if it engaged both entities in concrete partnerships that leverage their relationships with the states beyond the current information-sharing activities by OJJDP. Both entities have the opportunity to incorporate not only the recommendations of the 2013 NRC report but also the recommendations of the Youth Engagement Sub-Committee to include youth voice and engagement at the federal level. This presents another opportunity for OJJDP leadership in juvenile justice reform.

Law Enforcement Organizations

Partnerships with national law enforcement associations should be one of the centerpieces of OJJDP's efforts to transform how law enforcement deals with young offenders. These organizations represent the majority of the police executives across the nation; many of them have memberships that overlap, and all have the infrastructures already in place to reach and influence their members effectively. The organizations host national, regional, and local training forums. They possess the expertise, staffing, and networking to build and systematically deliver a sustainable program across the nation. Most important, they represent the part of the system where most diversion activities take place. As discussed in Chapter 2, developing and using alternatives to justice system involvement is one of the hallmarks of a developmental approach to reform.

Law enforcement agencies across the country have already recognized the important role they play in the juvenile justice system. In September 2013, the International Association of Chiefs of Police (IACP), with support from the MacArthur Foundation, conducted a survey of over 900 law enforcement executives. The survey found that these executives desired to be better informed on how to address the nation's youths, particularly through early intervention and diversion activities for justice-involved youths, as well as through improved interactions with them and their families (International Association of Chiefs of Police, 2013). For optimal results, any effort by OJJDP to engage with national law enforcement entities should be strategic, well defined, supported with funding and training and technical assistance, and built on existing activities.

An example of an ongoing effort to increase pre-arrest jail diversion is the Crisis Intervention Team (CIT) training developed by the Memphis, Tennessee, Police Department in 1988. The Memphis Police Department, working with members of the local Alliance for the Mentally Ill, designed CIT training that specifically trained officers to respond to incidents involving people with mental illness. The Memphis CIT model and other special-response approaches have been shown to be effective in reducing arrests of those with mental illness and improving the likelihood of treatment with community-based providers. This model took root across the nation, spreading to nearly 2,000 communities in more than 40 states and demonstrating the positive dividends of collaboration among law enforcement, mental health providers, advocates, and federal agencies such as SAMHSA and BJA (Council of State Governments' Criminal Justice/Mental Health Consensus Project, 2005; National Alliance on Mental Illness, 2012).[16]

---

[16]SAMHSA and BJA have funded initiatives that adopt this model, including SAMHSA's Law Enforcement and Behavioral Health Partnerships for Early Diversion grantees and the BJA-funded Council of State Governments' Criminal Justice/Mental Health Consensus Project. For the former, see http://gainscenter.samhsa.gov/earlydiversion/default.asp [August 2014]; for the latter, see Council of State Governments' Criminal Justice/Mental Health Consensus Project, 2005.

Standards for Juvenile Justice

Another potential collaborative opportunity for OJJDP is working with the American Bar Association (ABA) to revise and update the ABA's standards on juvenile justice, a stand-alone volume that supplements the ABA's influential *Standards on Criminal Justice* (American Bar Association, 1968). The original Juvenile Justice Standards Project was initiated in 1971 at the Institute of Judicial Administration (IJA) with the intention of annotating the *Standards for Criminal Justice* to identify how juvenile law diverged from law governing (adult) criminal adjudication. The IJA and ABA staffs found more extensive fundamental disparities than they had anticipated. In particular, the criminal justice standards did not address the issues presented by the separate courts and agencies established to handle problems affecting juveniles and their families. As reviewed by Shepherd (1996), IJA then began to plan

> . . . a modest project to produce a single volume devoted to juvenile justice. Ten years and 23 volumes later, the IJA-ABA *Juvenile Justice Standards* series was completed. . . . The House of Delegates [had] approved 17 volumes in 1979, and three more in August 1980. Of the remaining three volumes, Standards Relating to Schools and Education was withdrawn from consideration by the House of Delegates as too specialized; Standards Relating to Noncriminal Misbehavior volume was tabled by the delegates as too controversial; and Standards Relating to Abuse and Neglect was returned for revision. A revised volume on abuse and neglect was approved by the joint commission and published with the final revised drafts of all 23 IJA-ABA juvenile justice standards volumes in 1980. In 1992, the Juvenile Justice Committee of the Section on Criminal Justice formed a subcommittee to review and revive the standards, and that subcommittee . . . reported that they were still timely and singularly helpful. At the 1994 ABA Annual Meeting in New Orleans, the committee presented a Presidential Showcase Program on "Taking the ABA Juvenile Justice Standards to the 21st Century: Juvenile Justice Reform for the 90s." The audience was enthusiastic and plans were laid to publish a one-volume compilation of the standards with annotations to mark the body's intention to urge widespread implementation of the Standards.

In 2006, the Executive Committee of ABA's Criminal Justice Section approved work on an additional chapter to the *Juvenile Justice Standards* covering standards relating to crossover, dual-jurisdiction, and multisystem youths. These standards have not been finalized, and work on them continues. Drafts have been reviewed by the Criminal Justice Section's Standards Committee, and revisions are being made before presentation to the Criminal Justice Section Council.[17]

It has been almost 35 years since the ABA approved the *Juvenile Justice Standards*. Review and reconsideration are long overdue in light of developments in the law as well as advances in knowledge about adolescent development. The committee understands that the ABA's Criminal Justice Section Executive Committee is considering initiating a process to review and revise the existing juvenile justice standards. The committee hopes that the ABA will undertake this project and that it will convene a multidisciplinary task force to conduct the necessary study, with participation by the relevant professional, scientific, and stakeholder organizations, which should include a range of stakeholder groups such as the National Juvenile Defender Center, National Association of Counsel for Children, National District Attorneys Association, American Prosecutors Association, and National Association of Attorneys General. If the ABA does decide to undertake this project, DOJ, acting through OJJDP, should participate actively and provide its full support.

Recommendation 5-6: OJJDP, with support of the attorney general, should support and participate in an American Bar Association project to formulate a new and updated volume of standards for juvenile justice based on the developmental approach.

---

[17]Personal communication on juvenile standards from Kevin Scruggs, Director, Criminal Justice Standards Project, American Bar Association, to Richard Bonnie, Chair, Committee on a Prioritized Plan to Implement a Developmental Approach in Juvenile Justice Reform, July 2014.

OJJDP's Role

All of the national organizations discussed here actively work to influence policy and institutional changes on a national level. Effectively engaging these and other national organizations in the effort to reform the juvenile justice system may require OJJDP to (1) educate the leadership within these and other organizations on the hallmarks of the developmental approach, and (2) work with them on developing curriculum and training tools for their constituent agencies, including training tailored to the needs of agency leaders, management, and line staff/officers. The committee sees a clear partnership opportunity involving the CJJ and FACJJ to develop a training plan to ensure that each State Advisory Group participates in and completes the training curriculum (see discussion on training State Advisory Groups in Chapter 4).

Recommendation 5-7: OJJDP should increase its capacity to provide training and technical assistance by initiating or capitalizing on partnerships with national organizations that provide training and guidance to their membership and recognize the need for enhanced training in the hallmarks of a developmental approach to juvenile justice reform.

FAMILY AND YOUTH PARTNERSHIPS

Chapter 2 highlights the evidence that familial involvement throughout the juvenile justice system process is likely to be conducive to successful outcomes and reduced re-offending. Currently, family engagement is viewed in juvenile justice from the individual case/response perspective, which focuses on decision making and planning on a case-by-case basis. Pennell and colleagues (2011) noted that while there is limited empirical evidence regarding the specific correlation with outcomes in the juvenile justice system, this type of engagement has resulted in greater client satisfaction in both the child welfare and juvenile justice systems. As they summarized their position: "Families know what works for them" (Pennell et al., 2011, p. 43).

As the understanding of family engagement has evolved, a new opportunity for youths and families, particularly legacy families, has emerged. Selected system-involved youths and their family members can now be viewed as full and equal partners in the system itself. Like other partners, system-involved youths and families, including legacy families, can provide direct and meaningful input into discussions on system improvements, policies, programs, and practices that may affect all system-involved youths (Pennell et al., 2011).

OJJDP can be the champion for both family and youth engagement and partnership as it implements the developmental approach to juvenile justice reform. To do so, it could build on recommendations in the 2011 report from the Center for Juvenile Justice Reform, *Safety, Fairness, & Stability for Youth and Families: Recommendations to Strengthen Federal Agency Support of Family Engagement Efforts,* and on the experiences of SAMHSA's Systems of Care in mental health services (Pennell et al., 2011). Other sources to draw upon include the IDEA [Individuals with Disabilities Education Act] Resource Centers for education and for family group conferencing in child welfare, as well as initiatives such as those undertaken by Pennsylvania as a Models for Change site. The committee has already recommended a few first-step actions OJJDP can take to move family and youth engagement and partnerships forward (see Recommendations 4-1 and 5-3 and the implementation plan in Chapter 6).

FOUNDATION PARTNERSHIPS

As noted throughout this report, OJJDP has a number of opportunities to work with foundations to develop public-private partnerships that could work collaboratively to: (1) develop and invest in pilot programs, (2) jointly fund established programs, (3) support capacity building for staff or grantees, (4) convene experts and stakeholders, (5) educate the public and members of the policy community, (6) fund research and policy analysis, and (7) evaluate policy and program implementation (Abramson et al., 2012). In the example of the Neighborhood Revitalization Initiative, the federal agencies pooled resources or coordinated existing grants to support the Promise Neighborhood Program. In a parallel effort, a group of foundations separately pooled their resources to fund the technical assistance and training element of a similar grant program entitled the Promise Neighborhoods Institute.

Ten foundations[18] supported the full range of training and technical assistance to the federal grantees, from Web-based resources and trainings to onsite long-term technical assistance.

OJJDP could, for instance, engage in a partnership with a foundation and a national association to identify and address the specific training needs of a specific constituency. An example of this approach is already under way with the IACP and the MacArthur Foundation, with OJJDP support. In June of 2011, the IACP entered into a multiyear project with the MacArthur Foundation to increase the leadership role of state and local law enforcement executives in addressing juvenile justice issues. One of the primary goals for establishing this partnership, called "Law Enforcement's Leadership Role in the Advancement of Promising Practices in Juvenile Justice," is to identify opportunities for law enforcement executives to build partnerships and advance innovative approaches to dealing with juvenile offenders in the areas they serve. Through this partnership an advisory group was established, focus group meetings were held, and a national survey was completed. A national summit on law enforcement leadership in juvenile justice was held September 2013. In 2014, a 4-day training institute will be launched to train law enforcement agencies across the country on tools to respond to youthful offenders (International Association of Chiefs of Police, 2011).[19] This approach could be strengthened by drawing from a curriculum based on the hallmarks of a developmental approach.

However, it is important to note that foundation-government partnerships are as fraught with challenges as the other partnerships discussed throughout this chapter. The Council on Foundations has provided guidance for such collaborative partnerships due to the potential for culture clash and misunderstandings that may result when two such different entities attempt to work together on a joint project. OJJDP would be well served if leadership and staff enhanced their understanding of these differences in order to strengthen their ability to capitalize and leverage these vital relationships (Abramson et al., 2012).

---

[18]The ten contributors were the Annie E. Casey Foundation, George Kaiser Family Foundation, JP Morgan Chase Foundation, Robert Wood Johnson Foundation, Atlantic Philanthropies, Ford Foundation, The California Endowment, W.K. Kellogg Foundation, Walmart Foundation, and the Open Society Institute.

[19]See also International Association of Chiefs of Police. *Advancing Juvenile Justice in Law Enforcement.* Available: http://www.theiacp.org/Advancing-Juvenile-Justice-in-Law-Enforcement [May 2014].

6

The Path Forward

Previous chapters of this report have set forth a blueprint for the federal government to facilitate juvenile justice reform in states, localities, and tribal jurisdictions based on a developmental approach. In Chapters 3 through 5, the committee made recommendations for the U.S. Department of Justice (DOJ) and the Office of Juvenile Justice and Delinquency Prevention (OJJDP). In this chapter, the committee responds directly to the agency's request for an explicit roadmap by restating those previous recommendations specifically directed to OJJDP and adding prioritized action steps for each recommendation. First we present the recommendations and action steps aimed at improving OJJDP's internal capacity to guide system reform. Then we outline the recommendations and associated action steps aimed at OJJDP's efforts to assist state, local, and tribal jurisdictions and to collaborate with national organizations to promote reform. The action steps have been broken down into Years 1, 2, and 3 (with corresponding fiscal years [FY], assuming Year 1 begins in fiscal year 2015), to provide the OJJDP administrator and leadership with the temporal road map for implementation they requested.

RECOMMENDATIONS AND ACTION STEPS

A successful transformation effort will require that the OJJDP administrator and executive staff build internal capacity and garner external support from other agencies in the federal government, foundations, and national organizations. In addition, the administrator and executive staff will need to embark immediately upon a process of modifying policies and addressing staffing issues, possibly using the recent example of the Federal Bureau of Investigation's transformation as a guide (Office of the Inspector General, 2004; U.S. General Accounting Office, 2003).

The committee stresses the need for OJJDP staff and leadership to be fully engaged in guiding reforms in the field. OJJDP staff should guide the work and develop the changes needed in training and technical assistance (TTA) delivery, solicitations, grant monitoring, etc. As noted in Chapter 3, changing the organization involves managing the climate as well as the process. This will require involving employees at all levels of the agency in the discussions and decisions about the process for implementing change. The first step, to be taken personally by the OJJDP administrator, will be to create a Change Management Team with representatives of every part of the agency. This team will work with the administrator to implement the action steps. The administrator and Change Management Team should anticipate that agency staff will express and experience a range of reactions to the changes that follow. The team should be prepared to engage staff throughout the organization by broadly sharing the rationale for and the scope of the changes, as well as how it will affect staff. This will require the administrator and Change Management Team to develop a full understanding of existing, as well as changing, structures, personnel, and culture within the organization.

The administrator should also immediately form a group of external advisers—a Transition Advisory Group—to assist with implementation as outlined below. External consultants and advisers are necessary to the transition phase, as they will bring specific knowledge and expertise in adolescent development, family engagement, racial disparities, data collection, research methodology, and curriculum development that will inform the work of the agency staff. However, consultants and advisers cannot be a substitute for staff by performing staff functions or providing leadership. For these reforms to be durable over time, it will be necessary for the staff of OJJDP to cultivate necessary staff expertise and become the leaders of change.

Improving Internal Capacity

Recommendation 3-1: OJJDP should develop a staff training curriculum based on the hallmarks of a developmental approach to juvenile justice reform. With the assistance of a team of external experts, it should implement the training curriculum on an ongoing basis and train, assign, or hire staff to align its capabilities with the skills and expertise needed to carry out a developmentally oriented approach to juvenile justice reform.

Action Steps for Recommendation 3-1		
Year 1 (FY 2015)	**Year 2 (FY 2016)**	**Year 3 (FY 2017)**
Create an external advisory group (the Transition Advisory Group) to work with an intra-agency team of staff and leadership at all levels of OJJDP (the Change Management Team) to develop, within 3-5 months, a curriculum to inform all professional staff about (1) advances in developmental science and their implications for juvenile justice system improvement and (2) the hallmarks of a developmental approach.	Develop staff evaluation measures and goals that align with the skills needed to drive a developmentally appropriate juvenile justice reform agenda.	Ensure that an accountability process is in place to evaluate staff on measures and goals.
Within 6 months, using the curriculum, initiate an agency-wide training activity to train staff on the developmental approach.	Review and evaluate the training curriculum to assess quality and impact.	Incorporate lessons learned in updated training programs.
Within 9 months, train, assign, and hire staff with appropriate skills and knowledge aligned with the goals of implementing a developmental approach.	Continue training and reinforce on an ongoing basis at staff meetings and seminars.	Continue training on an ongoing basis and routinely assess skills and knowledge of staff.
Develop partnerships with other federal agencies; state, local, and tribal governments; universities; or foundations to engage expert staff through the use of interagency agreements, details, and Intergovernmental Personnel Act (IPA) authority.	Implement partnerships with other federal agencies; state, local, and tribal governments; universities; or foundations to engage expert staff through interagency agreements, details, and IPA authority.	Continue use of interagency agreements, details, and IPA authority to maintain the necessary level of expertise on staff.
Following the training of key staff, re-examine all grant making, guidance, and leadership activities to identify specifically how to introduce or strengthen developmentally appropriate reforms that include approaches for ensuring compliance with core protections, including those described in Recommendation 4-5.	Implement changes in all grant making, guidance, and leadership activities to ensure that developmentally appropriate reforms become integral to all core activities, including ensuring compliance with core protections. Assign responsibility to staff along with accountability measures.	Continue and evaluate.
Not applicable.	Establish a mechanism for monitoring progress on agency transformation.	Review and assess progress annually.

Recommendation 3-2: OJJDP should establish a better balance between grant monitoring and system reform efforts by examining more efficient ways to monitor grants and compliance with the core protections from the JJDPA.

Action Steps for Recommendation 3-2		
Year 1 (FY 2015)	Year 2 (FY 2016)	Year 3 (FY 2017)
In the first 3 months, re-examine the grant monitoring systems to determine less resource-intensive options. Within 6 months, develop a grant management process that uses either (1) a random audit of representative samples and in-depth reviews of selected programs, (2) a rotating schedule of full reviews with monitoring or remediation plans in the intervening years, (3) a process of contracting out the monitoring functions, or (4) other possible methods.	Institute a new grant monitoring system.	Continue and evaluate.
Consistent with Recommendation 4-4, develop a competitive grant process for the demonstration project, predicated upon documented compliance with core protections.	Continue to monitor compliance with the core protections as part of demonstration project implementation.	Continue and evaluate.

Recommendation 3-3: OJJDP should take a leadership role in local, state, and tribal jurisdictions with respect to the development and implementation of administrative data systems by providing model formats for system structure, standards, and common definitions of data elements. OJJDP should also provide consultation on data systems as well as opportunities for sharing information across jurisdictions.

Action Steps for Recommendation 3-3		
Year 1 (FY 2015)	Year 2 (FY 2016)	Year 3 (FY 2017)
Within 6 months, develop model formats for collecting data regarding juvenile offenders, juvenile offending, and positive youth development.	Convene meetings with localities that have made sufficient progress in order to facilitate the exchange of information about innovative data practices, management, and organization.	Review and evaluate.
Following the development of the model formats, compile and share information regarding effective data collection practices and uses across localities, states, and tribal jurisdictions.	Continue to compile and share information.	Continue to compile and share information.
Work with other governmental agencies (e.g., Bureau of Justice Statistics, National Institutes of Health) whose data collection mechanisms may complement efforts central to OJJDP's mission to promote a developmental perspective.	Document partnership outcomes.	Analyze and reevaluate.

Recommendation 3-4: OJJDP should focus research efforts toward specific projects related to a developmental perspective on juvenile justice, capitalizing on an integration of its research and program efforts.

Action Steps for Recommendation 3-4		
Year 1 (FY 2015)	**Year 2 (FY 2016)**	**Year 3 (FY 2017)**
Initiate ad hoc research groups, composed of OJJDP staff as well as external researchers, to identify within 6 months priority research centered on a developmental perspective.	Continue using the ad hoc groups to review and update priority research areas.	Continue using the ad hoc groups to review and update priority research areas. Evaluate progress and research objectives.
Following the identification of priority research, develop research Requests for Proposals (RFPs), solicitations, and funding opportunities with language specific to a developmental perspective.	Issue research RFPs, solicitations, and funding opportunities that incorporate language specific to a developmental perspective.	Continue to ensure that research RFPs, solicitations, and funding opportunities incorporate language specific to a developmental perspective. Reassess on an ongoing basis.
Develop common outcome measures for research RFPs recommended by an ad hoc research group for data collection and research.	Issue RFPs that require researchers to use common outcome measures recommended by the ad hoc research group for data collection and research.	Continue and reassess on an ongoing basis.
Recruit staff with research and practice experience regarding developmental science.	Continue to recruit and retain staff with research and practice experience regarding developmental science.	Continue to recruit.
Develop research practitioner partnerships and visiting fellowships to contribute to the setting of research agendas regarding appropriate basic and applied research.	Promote research practitioner partnerships and visiting fellowships to contribute to the setting of research agendas regarding appropriate basic and applied research.	Continue to promote.

Assisting External Entities to Promote Reform

Recommendation 4-1: OJJDP should promote the development and strengthening of the State Advisory Groups (SAGs) to be juvenile justice reform leaders by supporting meaningful family and youth engagement, fostering partnerships, delivering strategic training and technical assistance aimed at facilitating reform, and ensuring that SAG members and staff are knowledgeable about the hallmarks of a developmental approach to juvenile justice.

Action Steps for Recommendation 4-1		
Year 1 (FY 2015)	**Year 2 (FY 2016)**	**Year 3 (FY 2017)**
As part of the curriculum developed under Recommendation 3-3 and in consultation with stakeholders, ensure that the curriculum being developed can be used to inform all stakeholders (including SAGs) about advances in developmental science and their implications for juvenile justice system improvement.	With the Transition Advisory Group, develop a methodology to verify satisfactory completion and use of the curriculum.	Verify that all SAG members are trained in the OJJDP curriculum on developmental science and corresponding juvenile justice system practices.
Develop standards for the hiring and training of staff who serve the SAGs, based on the hallmarks of a developmental approach.	Issue guidance for hiring SAG staff based on the standards.	Verify that SAGs are implementing the guidance for the hiring of staff.

Recommendation 4-2: OJJDP should develop a portfolio of training and technical assistance, properly balanced to be both strategic and tactical, to support the implementation of a developmental approach to juvenile justice reform. OJJDP should coordinate with agencies and organizations proficient in providing training and technical assistance based on the hallmarks of a developmental approach to juvenile justice reform. This proficiency should include historical experience working in system improvement efforts.

Recommendation 4-3: All applicants for technical assistance or demonstration grants sponsored by OJJDP should be required to show how they would use the assistance, either strategically or tactically, to implement or strengthen a developmental approach to juvenile justice reform.

Action Steps for Recommendations 4-2 and 4-3		
Year 1 (FY 2015)	**Year 2 (FY 2016)**	**Year 3 (FY 2017)**
Based upon the curriculum developed pursuant to Recommendation 3-3, require providers of training and technical assistance (TTA) to demonstrate mastery of a developmental approach.	Require TTA providers selected in Year 1 to demonstrate knowledge of the jurisdiction where they are to be deployed. Ensure that TTA providers are able to facilitate connections among jurisdictions with similar issues.	Continue and evaluate for success in accomplishing intended purpose.
Consistent with Recommendation 3-4, establish a competitive process to evaluate applicants for strategic or targeted technical assistance, based on excellence of the application and readiness to engage in reform.	Implement a competitive process to evaluate applicants for strategic or targeted technical assistance based on the excellence of the application and readiness to engage in reform.	Continue and evaluate for success in accomplishing intended purpose.
As part of the curriculum development under Recommendation 3-3, create guides for TTA work plans that have concrete objectives, strategies to be employed, outcomes, progress measures, and timelines.	Require TTA providers to implement the guides for TTA work plans that have concrete objectives, strategies to be employed, outcomes, progress measures, and timelines.	Continue and evaluate for success in accomplishing intended purpose.
Develop an evaluation plan for assessing the impact of implementing the developmental perspective in localities and states.	Begin data collection for the evaluation plan for assessing the impact of implementing the developmental perspective in localities and states.	Conduct the evaluation and continue annually.

Recommendation 4-4: OJJDP should establish new approaches for identifying racial and ethnic disparities across the juvenile justice system, promulgate new guidelines for reducing and eliminating racial and ethnic disparities, build the internal capacity and/or establish partnerships for assisting states with these new requirements, and strengthen the role of State Advisory Groups (SAGs) in monitoring the new guidelines by providing training and technical assistance to SAGs.

Action Steps for Recommendation 4-4		
Year 1 (FY 2015)	**Year 2 (FY 2016)**	**Year 3 (FY 2017)**
Within 6 months, issue new guidelines for reducing racial disparities.	Review and assess impact of racial disparities guidelines.	Review and assess impact of guidelines.
Within 12 months, create recommendations for data collection systems for each of the justice system decision points, disaggregated by race, ethnicity, and gender.	Require jurisdictions to implement data collection systems for each of the decision points, disaggregated by race, ethnicity, and gender; submit the data to OJJDP and develop plans for reducing disparities at the decision points where disparities are apparent from the data.	Collect and evaluate the outcomes of the plans.
Within 12 months, working with the Transition Advisory Group and training and technical assistance (TTA) providers, establish training program for State Agency Groups (SAGs) on new racial disparities guidelines.	Provide TTA to SAGs in monitoring the new guidelines.	Continue and assess efficacy of TTA program.
As part of development of a data collection template and new guidelines on racial disparities, establish a process for phasing out use of the Relative Rate Index (RRI).	Provide guidance to jurisdictions on phasing out use of the RRI.	Begin to phase out use of the RRI in favor of new measures in the template (disaggregated data by decision points).

Recommendation 4-5: In partnership with other federal agencies and the philanthropic community, OJJDP should develop a multiyear demonstration project designed to provide substantial technical assistance and financial support to selected states and localities to develop a comprehensive plan for reforming the state's juvenile justice system based on a developmental approach. The demonstration grant should include a requirement for strategies that reduce racial and ethnic disparities and the unnecessary use of confinement as well as other hallmarks of a developmental approach. OJJDP should ensure that State Advisory Group (SAG) members in states with demonstration sites are intimately involved in their state's pilot projects and help disseminate lessons learned to other states' SAGs.

Action Steps for Recommendation 4-5		
Year 1 (FY 2015)	**Year 2 (FY 2016)**	**Year 3 (FY 2017)**
Within 6 months, develop partnership with foundations. Within 12 months develop, in partnership with foundations, a multiyear demonstration grant program that incorporates the hallmarks of the developmental approach, emphasizes strategies to reduce racial and ethnic disparities, and includes a training and technical assistance component.	Launch a demonstration project in selected states and localities that have demonstrated an ability and willingness to accomplish multisystem initiatives to incorporate the hallmarks of the developmental approach into a reform effort of the juvenile justice system, including strategies to reduce racial and ethnic disparities.	Assess and evaluate the development, implementation, and lessons learned that enhance the tenets of a developmentally focused reform. Continue to add cohorts of demonstration grantees as the program is taken to scale.

Recommendation 5-2: OJJDP should initiate and support collaborative partnerships at the federal, state, local, and tribal levels and should use them strategically to advance the goal of a developmentally appropriate juvenile justice system.

Action Steps for Recommendation 5-2		
Year 1 (FY 2015)	Year 2 (FY 2016)	Year 3 (FY 2017)
As part of training OJJDP staff and management, include federal agency leaders, management, and staff in training about advances in developmental science and the implications for system-involved youths.	Work with federal agency partners to integrate federal programs and target resources, as appropriate, in coordinated grant strategies, and to provide joint training and technical assistance and shared best practices using the developmental approach.	Continue, assess, and evaluate.

Recommendation 5-3: OJJDP should establish and convene, on an ongoing basis, a Family Advisory Group to the Coordinating Council on Juvenile Justice and Delinquency Prevention, composed of youths and families whose lives have been impacted by the juvenile justice system.

Action Steps for Recommendation 5-3		
Year 1 (FY 2015)	Year 2 (FY 2016)	Year 3 (FY 2017)
Within 3 months, work with members of the Coordinating Council on Juvenile Justice and Delinquency Prevention to formally establish a Youth and Family Advisory Group to the council. Within 6 months, work with the council and identified stakeholder groups to secure nominations for the Youth and Family Advisory Group. By 12 months, fully establish the new group and convene its first meeting.	Within 6 months, work with the new Youth and Family Advisory Group for recommendations of two system-involved youths and two members of system-involved or legacy families to represent the Youth and Family Advisory Group on the coordinating council or to serve as liaisons. Work with the Youth and Family Advisory Group on a formal process for nominating members to the coordinating council and for providing advice to the coordinating council on all matters related to the juvenile justice system.	Continue to implement a process for representation of the Youth and Family Advisory Group in all relevant coordinating council deliberations.
Work with the Youth and Family Advisory Group to develop and implement a training program for coordinating council members on mechanisms for creating and embedding family-focused policies and practices to institutionalize the active and meaningful involvement of family members.	Develop a methodology to monitor and evaluate the training program; make changes as needed to institutionalize the active and meaningful involvement of family members.	Use methodology to monitor and evaluate.

Recommendation 5-4: OJJDP, with the support of the Attorney General, should use the Coordinating Council on Juvenile Justice and Delinquency Prevention strategically to implement key components of developmentally oriented juvenile justice reform through interagency, intergovernmental (federal-state-local partnering), and public-private partnering activities with specific measurable objectives.

Action Steps for Recommendation 5-4		
Year 1 (FY 2015)	**Year 2 (FY 2016)**	**Year 3 (FY 2017)**
Within 6 months, work with all members of the coordinating council to develop a strategic plan for collectively improving outcomes for system-involved youths. Based upon the hallmarks of a developmental approach, outline a plan that defines a common outcome; establishes joint strategies; leverages resources; outlines agreed-upon roles and responsibilities; establishes compatible policies and procedures; and develops mechanisms to monitor, evaluate, and report on results. Within 12 months, disseminate the plan to all stakeholders and begin to work with each member of the council to issue guidance on implementation of the plan.	To monitor, evaluate, and report on results derived from coordinating council engagement, work with members of the council to reinforce agency accountability for collaborative efforts through agency plans, reports, and outcome measures; reinforce individual accountability through performance management systems. Work with each agency, through the coordinating council, to publicly issue reports on progress based upon the accountability measures.	Continue, assess, and evaluate.

Recommendation 5-5: OJJDP should work with its federal agency and Coordinating Council on Juvenile Justice and Delinquency Prevention partners (i) to blend or leverage available federal funds to support OJJDP demonstration projects and (ii) to provide guidance to eligible grantees on leveraging federal funding at the state or local level.

Action Steps for Recommendation 5-5		
Year 1 (FY 2015)	**Year 2 (FY 2016)**	**Year 3 (FY 2017)**
Consistent with Recommendation 4-4, within 6 months work with members of the coordinating council to review the rules and requirements for all relevant federal funding streams. Within 9 months, identify mechanisms to blend or leverage funding to support the demonstration project. Within 12 months, establish necessary interagency agreements.	Consistent with Recommendation 4-4 launch a demonstration project in selected states and localities. Review implementation of blended or leveraged funding mechanisms, improve as needed.	Continue to identify opportunities for blending, assess implementation, improve as needed.
Within 12 months, work with members of the coordinating council to develop guidance for grantees on the allowable blending and leveraging of federal funding streams.	Issue guidance to the grantees with members of the coordinating council. Reassess guidance as part of review process, improve as needed.	Continue to assess and improve guidance as needed.

Recommendation 5-6: OJJDP, with support of the attorney general, should support and participate in an American Bar Association project to formulate a new and updated volume of standards for juvenile justice based on the developmental approach.

Action Steps for Recommendation 5-6		
Year 1 (FY 2015)	**Year 2 (FY 2016)**	**Year 3 (FY 2017)**
Collaborate with the American Bar Association (ABA) to begin plans for a review and update of the *Standards for Juvenile Justice*. Work with ABA to select and appoint members of a task force.	Participate in and support the task force in collaboration with the ABA.	Continue participation. Disseminate draft standards for review and support completion in subsequent years, if process is not completed during Year 3.
Provide support including funding as appropriate.	Continue support, including funding as appropriate.	Continue support, including funding as appropriate.

Recommendation 5-7: OJJDP should increase its capacity to provide training and technical assistance by initiating or capitalizing on partnerships with national organizations that provide training and guidance to their membership and recognize the need for enhanced training in the hallmarks of a developmental approach to juvenile justice reform.

Action Steps for Recommendation 5-7		
Year 1 (FY 2015)	**Year 2 - FY (2016)**	**Year 3 (FY 2017)**
Consistent with Recommendation 4-2, develop partnerships with national organizations that participate in training and demonstrate mastery of the developmental approach. With national partners, develop a strategy for targeted training and technical assistance (TTA) for decision makers at all juvenile justice decision points.	Continue developing and sustaining partnerships; continue implementing strategy for targeting TTA to decision makers.	Continue developing and sustaining partnerships; continue implementing strategy for targeting TTA to decision makers.
As part of the curriculum developed under Recommendation 3-3, ensure the development of a curriculum tailored to individual stakeholders' particular decision point(s) that communicates developmental science and its implications for that stakeholder's role in juvenile justice system improvement.	Initiate training activities for stakeholder groups on the curriculum.	Review and evaluate the training curriculum to determine success in accomplishing the intended purpose.

CONCLUSION

The committee notes that if this prioritized plan is implemented over the next 3 years as outlined, the developmental approach should be fully embedded in the organization's culture at the end of that period. The agency should then be well positioned to facilitate and sustain support for reforming the juvenile justice system based on the hallmarks of a developmental approach:

1. Accountability Without Criminalization;
2. Alternatives to Justice System Involvement;
3. Individualized Response Based on Assessment of Needs and Risks;
4. Confinement Only When Necessary for Public Safety;
5. A Genuine Commitment to Fairness;

6. Sensitivity to Disparate Treatment; and
7. Family Engagement.

Reform of the nation's juvenile justice systems grounded in advancing knowledge about adolescent development is a widely supported goal, crossing the usual lines of political disagreement. The 2013 NRC report summarized the scientific foundation for a developmental approach to reform and distilled its implications for reform. This report sets forth a detailed and prioritized strategic plan for the federal government to support and facilitate developmentally oriented juvenile justice reform. The chapters lay out a plan for OJJDP to accomplish three key tasks: organizing itself and setting its priorities so that it has the capacity and commitment to carry out its mission; providing guidance and support to enable states, tribal entities, and localities to reform their juvenile justice systems based on a developmental approach; and forging the partnerships that will be needed to achieve and sustain developmentally based reform.

System change in juvenile justice necessitates a shared commitment among the various actors and stakeholders to the goal of reform based on a developmentally informed approach. Adequate funding is of course necessary to hire and retain well-qualified staff at all levels of the organization and system—staff who have been trained on adolescent development and are immersed in a culture that embraces the hallmarks of a developmental approach.

The available literature recognizes that system change is a complex process and involves a long-term commitment from the organization as change agent and from its personnel. The committee believes that for OJJDP to succeed in redefining itself as an agent for juvenile justice reform, it will require support for the change from its parent agencies within DOJ; the intellectual, technological, and financial resources needed to carry out this change; and the ability to mobilize staff and manage them throughout the overhaul process. The vision for juvenile justice reform must eventually permeate all things that the organization does. The pivotal component of the plan is to strengthen the role, capacity, and commitment of OJJDP, the lead federal agency in the field. By carrying out the recommendations in this report, the federal government will both reaffirm and advance the promise of the Juvenile Justice and Delinquency Prevention Act.

References

Abramson, A., Soskis, B., and Toeple, S. (2012). *Public-Philanthropic Partnerships in the U.S.: A Literature Review of Recent Experiences.* Arlington, VA: Council on Foundations. Available: http://www.cof.org/sites/default/files/documents/files/GMU-PPP%20Lit%20Review.pdf [May 2014].

Advancement Project. (2014). *Ending the Schoolhouse to Jailhouse Track: Clayton County, GA.* Available: http://safequalityschools.org/pages/clayton-county-ga. [April 2014].

Allen-Hagen, B. (1991). *Public Juvenile Facilities: Children in Custody 1989.* Washington, DC: Office of Juvenile Justice and Delinquency Prevention, U.S. Department of Justice.

American Academy of Child and Adolescent Psychiatry. (2012). *Solitary Confinement of Juvenile Offenders.* Available: http://www.aacap.org/cs/root/policy_statements/solitary_confinement_of_juvenile_offenders [August 2012].

American Bar Association. (1968). *Standards on Criminal Justice.* Washington, DC: Author.

American Civil Liberties Union. (2013). *Alone & Afraid: Children Held in Solitary Confinement and Isolation in Juvenile Detention and Correctional Facilities.* New York: Author.

Annie E. Casey Foundation. (2013). *Juvenile Detention Alternatives Initiative: 2012 Annual Results Report.* Baltimore, MD: Author. Available: http://www.aecf.org/m/resourcedoc/AECF-JDAI2012AnnualResultsReport-2013.pdf#page=4 [July 2014].

Aos, S., Lieb, R., Mayfield, J., Miller, M., and Pennucci, A. (2004). *Benefits and Costs of Prevention and Early Intervention Programs for Youth.* Olympia: Washington State Institute for Public Policy.

Austin, J., Cadora, E., Clear, T., Dansky, K., and Greene, J. (2013). *Ending Mass Incarceration: Charting a New Justice Reinvestment.* Washington, DC: The Sentencing Project. Available: http://sentencingproject.org/doc/Charting%20a%20New%20Justice%20Reinvestment%20FINAL.pdf [May 2014].

Austin, J., Johnson, K.D., and Gregorion, M. (2000). *Juveniles in Adult Prison and Jails: A National Assessment.* NCJ 182503. Washington, DC: U.S. Department of Justice, Bureau of Justice Assistance.

Bardach, E. (1998). *Getting Agencies to Work Together: The Practice and Theory of Managerial Craftsmanship.* Washington, DC: Brookings Institution Press.

Barnard, M. and Stoll, N. (2010). *Organizational Change Management: A Rapid Literature Review.* Short Policy Report No. 10/01. Bristol, United Kingdom: Centre for Understanding Behavior Change.

Barnoski, R.P. (2004). *Outcome Evaluation of Washington State's Research-based Programs for Juvenile Offenders.* Olympia: Washington State Institute for Public Policy.

Beck, A., Gilliard, D.K., Greenfeld, L.A., Harrell, C.W., Hester, T., Jankowski, L., Morton, D.C., Snell, T.L., and Stephan, J.J. (1993). *Survey of State Prison Inmates, 1991.* Washington, DC: U.S. Department of Justice, Bureau of Justice Statistics.

Beck, A.J., Cantor, D., Hartge, J., and Smith, T. (2013). *Sexual Victimization in Juvenile Facilities Reported by Youth, 2012.* NCJ 241708. Washington, DC: U.S. Department of Justice, Bureau of Justice Statistics.

Bishop, D.M., and Frazier, C. (2000). Consequences of transfer. In J. Fagan and F. Zimmerman (Eds.), *The Changing Borders of Juvenile Justice* (pp. 227-276). Chicago, IL: University of Chicago Press.

Brown, P., Pitt, J., and Hirota, J. (1999). *New Approaches to Technical Assistance: The Role of the Coach.* Chicago, IL: Chapin Hall Center for Children, University of Chicago.

Burns, B.J., Costello, E.J., Angold, A., Tweed, D., Stangl, D., Farmer, E.M.Z., and Erkanli, A. (1995). Children's mental health service use across service sectors. *Health Affairs 14*(3), 147-159.

Butts, J.A., and Evans, D.N. (2011, September). *Resolution, Reinvestment, and Realignment: Three Strategies for Changing Juvenile Justice.* New York: Research and Evaluation Center, John Jay College of Criminal Justice.

Butts, J.A., and Roman, J.K. (2014). *Line Drawing: Raising the Minimum Age of Criminal Court Jurisdiction in New York.* Research and Evaluation Center, John Jay College of Criminal Justice. February. Available: http://johnjayresearch.org/rec/files/2014/02/linedrawing.pdf [May 2014].

Caldwell, M.F., Skeem, J., Salekin, R., and Rybroek, G.V. (2006). Treatment response of adolescent offenders with psychopathy features: A 2-year follow-up. *Criminal Justice and Behavior, 33*(5), 571-596.

Caldwell, M.F., Vitacco, M., and Van Rybroek, G.J. (2006). Are violent delinquents worth treating? A cost-benefit analysis. *Journal of Research in Crime and Delinquency, 43*(2), 148-168.

Center for Children's Advocacy. (2013a, January). Reducing disproportionate minority contact (DMC) in the juvenile justice system: CCA project gaining state and national recognition. *Center for Children's Advocacy Newsletter.* Available: http://www.kidscounsel.org/january-2013-newsletter/ [July 2014].

Center for Children's Advocacy. (2013b). *Preventing School PushOut and Its Devastating Effect on African American Students in Connecticut's Poorest Cities.* Hartford, CT: Center for Children's Advocacy. Available: http://www.kidscounsel.org/preventing-school-pushout/ [April 2014].

Child Trends. (n.d.). *Juvenile Detention.* Available: http://www.childtrends.org/?indicators=juvenile-detention [July 2013].

Council of State Governments' Criminal Justice/Mental Health Consensus Project. (2005). *Law Enforcement/Mental Health Partnership Program.* Under cooperative agreement #2005 MU XK208 awarded by the Bureau of Justice Assistance. Washington, DC: Bureau of Justice Assistance. Available: http://www.pacenterofexcellence.pitt.edu/documents/Lawenforcementonepager.pdf [May 2014].

Davis, A., Irvine, A., and Ziedenberg, J. (2014). *Stakeholders' Views on the Movement to Reduce Youth Incarceration.* Washington, DC: National Council on Crime and Delinquency. Available: http://nccdglobal.org/sites/default/files/publication_pdf/deincarceration-summary-report.pdf [April 2014].

Dawson, K., and Berry, M. (2002). Engaging families in child welfare services: An evidence-based approach to best practice. *Child Welfare, 81*(2), 293-317.

Denhardt, R.B., and Denhardt, J.V. (1999). *Leadership for Change: Case Studies in American Local Government.* Washington, DC: IBM Centre for the Business of Government.

Ezell, M.E. (2007). The effect of criminal history variables on the process of desistance in adulthood among serious youthful offenders. *Journal of Contemporary Criminal Justice, 23*(1), 28-49.

Fabelo, T., Thompson, M.D., Plotkin, M., Carmichael, D., Marchbanks III, M., and Booth, E. (2011). *Breaking Schools' Rules: A Statewide Survey of How School Discipline Relates to Students' Success and Juvenile Justice Involvement.* New York: Council of State Governments and Public Policy Research Institute at Texas A&M University.

Fernandez, R. and Rainey, H.G. (2006). Managing successful organizational change in the public sector: An agenda for research practice. *Public Administration Review, 66*(2),168-176.

Feyerherm, W. (2011). Measuring DMC: The origins and use of the relative rate index. In N.Y. Parsons-Pollard (Ed.), *Disproportionate Minority Contact: Current Issues and Policies* (pp. 35-50). Durham, NC: Carolina Academic Press.

Feyerherm, W., Snyder, H.N., and Villarruel, F. (2009). Identification and monitoring. Chapter 1 in *Disproportionate Minority Contact Technical Assistance Manual* (4th ed.) Washington, DC: U.S. Department of Justice, Office of Juvenile Justice and Delinquency Prevention.

Fixsen, D.L., Naoom, S.F., Blase, K.A., Friedman, R.M. and Wallace, F. (2005). *Implementation Research: A Synthesis of the Literature. National Implementation Research Network.* Tampa: University of South Florida.

Forst, M., Fagen, J., and Vivona, T.S. (1989). Youth in prisons and training schools: Perceptions and consequences of the treatment-custody dichotomy. *Juvenile and Family Court Journal, 40*(1),1-14.

Garet, M.S., Porter, A.C., Desimone, L., Birman, B.F., and Yoon, K.S. (2001). What makes professional development effective? Results from a national sample of teachers. *American Educational Research Journal, 38*(4), 915-945.

Goldman, H., Thelander, S., and Westrin, C-G. (2000). Organizing mental health services: An evidence-based approach. *Journal of Mental Health Policy and Economics, 3*, 69-75.

Graham v. Florida, 560 U.S. 48. (2010).

Grindle, M.S., and Hilderbrand, M.E. (1995). Building sustainable capacity in the public sector: What can be done? *Public Administration & Development, 15*, 5.

Grisso, T., Steinberg, L., Woolard, J., Cauffman, E., Scott, E., Graham, S., Lexcen, F., Reppucci, N.D., and Schwartz, R. (2003). Juveniles' competence to stand trial: A comparison of adolescents' and adults' capacities as trial defendants. *Law and Human Behavior, 27*(4), 333-363.

Harbert, A., Finnegan, D., and Tyler, N. (1997). Collaboration: A study of a children's initiative. *Administration in Social Work, 21*(3-4), 83-107.

Hayes, C. (2002). *Thinking Broadly: Financing Strategies for Comprehensive Child and Family Initiatives.* Washington, DC: The Finance Project.

Hayes, C. (2014). *Catalog of Federal Funding Sources: Youth with, At-Risk of, Juvenile Justice Involvement (ages 10-24 years), May 18, 2014.* Available: http://sites.nationalacademies.org/dbasse/claj/dbasse_088937 [August 2014].

Hinton Hoytt, E., Schirald, V., Smith, B., and Ziendenberg, J. (2001). *Pathways to Juvenile Detention Reform: Reducing Racial Disparities in Juvenile Detention.* Baltimore, MD: Annie E. Casey Foundation. Available: http://www.aecf.org/upload/publicationfiles/reducing%20racial%20disparities.pdf [May 2014].

Howell, J.C. (2009). *Preventing and Reducing Juvenile Delinquency: A Comprehensive Framework* (2nd ed.). Thousand Oaks, CA: Sage.

Institute of Medicine. (1994). *Reducing Risks for Mental Disorders: Frontiers for Preventive Intervention Research.* Washington, DC: National Academy Press.

International Association of Chiefs of Police. (2011). *Advancing Juvenile Justice in Law Enforcement.* Available: http://www.theiacp.org/Advancing-Juvenile-Justice-in-Law-Enforcement [May 2014].

International Association of Chiefs of Police. (2013). *Law Enforcement's Leadership Role in the Advancement of Promising Practices in Juvenile Justice: Executive Officer Survey Findings.* Alexandria, VA: MacArthur Foundation. Available: http://www.modelsforchange.net/publications/478 [May 2014].

Justice for Families. (2012). *Families Unlocking Futures: Solutions to the crisis in Juvenile Justice.* A Report by Justice for Families with research support by Datacenter. September. Available: http://www.justice4families.org/download-report/ [August 2014].

Kania, J., and Kramer, M. (2011). Collective impact. *Stanford Social Innovation Review, 67*, 36-41.

Kemp, S. P., Marcenko, M. O., Hoagwood, K., and Vesneski, W. (2009). Engaging parents in child welfare services: Bridging family needs and child welfare mandates. *Child Welfare, 88(1)*, 101-126.

Kline, S. (1989). *Children in Custody, 1975-85: Census of Public and Private Juvenile Detention, Correctional, and Shelter Facilities, 1975, 1977, 1979, 1983, and 1985.* NCJ 114065. Washington, DC: U.S. Department of Justice, Bureau of Justice Statistics.

Kotter, J.P. (1995). Leading change: Why transformation efforts fail. *Harvard Business Review, 73*(2), 59-67.

Kotter, J.P. (1996). *Leading Change.* Boston, MA: Harvard Business School Press.

LaVigne, N., Bieler, S., Ho, H., Mayer, D., Pacifici, L., Peterson, B., and Samuels. J. (2014). *Justice Reinvestment Initiative State Assessment Report.* Washington, DC: U.S. Department of Justice, Bureau of Justice Assistance and Urban Institute. Available: http://www.urban.org/UploadedPDF/412994-Justice-Reinvestment-Initiative-State-Assessment-Report.pdf [July 2014].

Marquis, C., and Tilcsik, A. (2013). Imprinting: Toward A Multilevel Theory. *Academy of Management Annals, 7*, 193-243; Harvard Business School Organizational Behavior Unit Working Paper No. 13-061; Rotman School of Management Working Paper No. 2198954. Available: http://papers.ssrn.com/sol3/papers.cfm?abstract_id=2198954 [July 2014].

Miller v. Alabama, 567 10-9646. (2012).

Moore, A. (2012). *California Cities Gang Prevention Network: Case Studies and Analysis of Local Funding Strategies.* Washington, DC: National League of Cities and National Council on Crime and Delinquency. Available: http://www.nlc.org/Documents/Find%20City%20Solutions/IYEF/Violence%20Prevention/YEF-ccgpn-case-studies-and-analysis-of-local-funding-strategies-june-2012.pdf [May 2014].

Morgan, E., Salomon, N., Plotkin, M., and Cohen, R. (2014). *The School Discipline Consensus Report: Strategies from the Field to Keep Students in School and Out of the Juvenile Justice System.* New York: Council of State Governments Justice Center. Available: http://csgjusticecenter.org/wp-content/uploads/2014/06/The_School_Discipline_Consensus_Report.pdf [July 2014].

Mulvey, E.P. (2005). Risk assessment in juvenile justice policy and practice. In K. Heilbrun, N.E. Goldstein, and R. Redding (Eds.), *Juvenile Delinquency: Prevention, Assessment, and Intervention* (pp. 209-232). New York: Oxford University Press.

Mulvey, E.P., and Iselin, A.R. (2008). Improving professional judgments of risk and amenability in juvenile justice. *Future of Children, 18*(2), 35-37.

National Alliance on Mental Illness. (2012). *CIT Toolkit CIT Facts.* Arlington, VA: National Alliance on Mental Illness. Available: http://www.nami.org/Content/ContentGroups/Policy/CIT/CIT_Facts_4.11.12.pdf [July 2014].

National Collaborative on Workforce and Disability for Youth. (2006, January). *Blending and Braiding Funds and Resources: The Intermediary as Facilitator.* Issue 18. Number #E-9-4-1-0070. Washington, DC: U.S. Department of Labor, Office of Disability Employment. Available: http://www.ncwd-youth.info/sites/default/files/infobrief_issue18.pdf [May 2014].

National Council on Crime and Delinquency. (2007). *And Justice for Some: Differential Treatment of Youth of Color in the Justice System.* Oakland, CA: Author.

National Evaluation and Technical Assistance Center. (2010). *Fact Sheet: Juvenile Justice Facilities.* Washington, DC: National Evaluation and Technical Assistance Center. Available: http://www.neglected-delinquent.org/sites/default/files/docs/factSheet_facilities.pdf [May 2014].

National Governors Association Center for Best Practices. (May 2004). *Early Lessons from States to Promote Youth Development.* Washington, DC: Author.

National Research Council. (2005). *Improving Evaluation of Anticrime Programs.* Committee on Improving Evaluation of Anti-Crime Programs. Committee on Law and Justice, Division of Behavioral and Social Sciences and Education. Washington, DC: The National Academies Press.

National Research Council. (2013). *Reforming Juvenile Justice: A Developmental Approach.* Committee on Assessing Juvenile Justice Reform. R.J. Bonnie, R.L. Johnson, B.M. Chemers, and J.A. Schuck (Eds.). Committee on Law and Justice, Division of Behavioral and Social Sciences and Education. Washington, DC: The National Academies Press.

National Research Council. (2014). *The Growth of Incarceration in the United States: Exploring Causes and Consequences.* Washington, DC: The National Academies Press.

National Research Council and Institute of Medicine. (2002). *Community Programs to Promote Youth Development.* Committee on Community-Level Programs for Youth. J. Eccles and J. A. Gootman (Eds.). Board on Children, Youth, and Families, Division of Behavioral and Social Sciences and Education. Washington, DC: National Academy Press.

National Research Council and Institute of Medicine. (2009). *Preventing Mental, Emotional, and Behavioral Disorders Among Young People: Progress and Possibilities.* Committee on the Prevention of Mental Disorders and Substance Abuse Among Children, Youth, and Young Adults: Research Advances and Promising Interventions. M.E. O'Connell, T. Boat, and K.E. Warner (Eds.). Board on Children, Youth, and Families, Division of Behavioral and Social Sciences and Education. Washington, DC: The National Academies Press.

New York Civil Liberties Union. (2013). *A, B, C, D, STPP: How School Discipline Feeds the School-to-Prison Pipeline.* New York: Author. Available: http://www.nyclu.org/files/publications/nyclu_STPP_1021_FINAL.pdf [July 2014].

Nuñez-Neto, B. (2008). *Juvenile Justice: Legislative History and Current Legislative Issues.* CRS Report for Congress RL33947. Washington, DC: Congressional Research Service, Library of Congress. Available: http://b.3cdn.net/naeh/b882bdf314773fa80d_eum6bhx8v.pdf [July 2014].

O'Donnell, L., Scattergood, P., Alder, M., San Doval, A., and Al, E. (2000). The role of technical assistance in the replication of effective HIV interventions. *AIDS Education and Prevention, 12*(Suppl. A), 99-111.

Office of Juvenile Justice and Delinquency Prevention. (1983). *Children in Custody: Advance Report on the 1982 Census of Public Juvenile Facilities.* Washington, DC: U.S. Department of Justice, Office of Juvenile Justice and Delinquency Prevention. Available: https://www.ncjrs.gov/App/publications/abstract.aspx?ID=93805 [July 2014].

Office of Juvenile Justice and Delinquency Prevention. (1995). *Guide for Implementing the Comprehensive Strategy for Serious, Violent, and Chronic Juvenile Offenders.* Washington, DC: U.S. Department of Justice, Office of Juvenile Justice and Delinquency Prevention, Office of Justice Programs.

Office of Juvenile Justice and Delinquency Prevention. (2012). *How OJJDP Is Working for Youth Justice and Safety—Annual Report.* NCJ 241584. Washington, DC: U.S. Department of Justice. Available: http://www.ojjdp.gov/pubs/241584.pdf [August 2014].

Office of Juvenile Justice and Delinquency Prevention. (2014). *OJJDP FY 2014 Title II Formula Grants Program.* CFDA #16.540. Washington, DC: U.S. Department of Justice. Available: http://www.ojjdp.gov/grants/solicitations/FY2014/TitleII.pdf [August 2014].

Office of the Inspector General. (2004, September). *The Internal Effects of the Federal Bureau of Investigation's Reprioritization.* Audit Report 04-39. Available: http://www.justice.gov/oig/reports/FBI/a0439/ch1.htm [May 2014]

Patti, R., Packard, T., Daly, D., Tucker-Tatlow, J., and Prosek, K. (2003). *Seeking Better Performance Through Interagency Collaboration: Prospects and Challenges.* San Diego: Southern Area Consortium of Human Services. Available: http://theacademy.sdsu.edu/Documents/SACHSIntegratedServicesResearchReport.pdf [May 2014].

Pennell, J., Shapiro, C., and Spigner, C. (2011). *Safety, Fairness, Stability: Repositioning Juvenile Justice and Child Welfare to Engage Families and Communities.* Washington, DC: Center for Juvenile Justice Reform. Available: http://cjjr. georgetown.edu/pdfs/famengagement/FamilyEngagementPaper.pdf [May 2014].

Piquero, A.R. (2008). Disproportionate minority contact. *The Future of Children, 18*(2), 59-79.

Poister, T.H., and Streib, G. (1999). Performance measurement in municipal government: Assessing the state of practice. *Public Administration Review 59*(4), 325-345.

Potter, C., and Brough, R. (2004). Systemic capacity building: A hierarchy of needs. *Health Policy and Planning, 19*(5), 336-345.

Puzzanchera, C., and Adams, B. (2011). *National Disproportionate Minority Contact Databook.* Washington, DC: Office of Juvenile Justice and Delinquency Prevention. Available: http://www.ojjdp.gov/ojstatbb/dmcdb/index.html [July 2014].

Puzzanchera, C., and Addie. S. (2014). *Delinquency Cases Waived to Criminal Court, 2010.* Washington, DC: Office of Juvenile Justice and Delinquency Prevention, U.S. Department of Justice. Available: http://www.ojjdp.gov/pubs/243042.pdf [April 2014].

Rappaport, A. (2013). Realigning California corrections. *Federal Sentencing Reporter,* 25(4), 216-217.

Ray, M.L., Wilson, M.M., Wandersman, A., Meyers, D.C., and Katz, J. (2012). Using a training-of-trainers approach and pro-active technical assistance to bring evidence based programs to scale: An operationalization of the interactive systems framework's support system. *American Journal of Community Psychology, 50*(3-4), 415-427.

Redding, R.E. (2008). Juvenile transfer laws: An effective deterrent to delinquency? *Juvenile Justice Bulletin.* Available: http://works.bepress.com/richard_redding/6 [August 2012].

Robertson, A. (2005). Including parents, foster parents and parenting caregivers in the assessments and interventions of young children placed in the foster care system. *Children and Youth Services Review, 28,* 180-192.

Roper v. Simmons, 543 U.S. 551. (2005).

Rust, B. (1999). DeCat in the hat: Iowa's first successful step toward devolving resources, responsibility, and accountability for child and family outcomes. *AdvoCasey: Documenting Programs That Work for Kids and Families,1*(1), 4-13. Available: http://files.eric.ed.gov/fulltext/ED438386.pdf [May 2014].

Scheffler, R., Zhang, A., and Snowden, L. (2001). Impact of realignment on utilization and cost of community-based mental health services in California. *Administration and Policy in Mental Health,* 29(2), 129-143. Available: http://download.springer.com/static/pdf/444/art%253A10.1023%252FA%253A1014336530490.pdf?auth66=1408636705_196af069cfbbb257057864e55fb14685&ext=.pdf [August 2014].

Scott, E.S., and Grisso, T. (2005). Developmental incompetence, due process, and juvenile justice policy. *North Carolina Law Review, 83*(4), 793-846.

Shepherd, Jr., R.E. (1996). JJ standards: Anchor in the storm. *Criminal Justice Magazine—American Bar Association.* 10 Crim. Just. 39 (1995-1996). Available: http://www.americanbar.org/publications/criminal_justice_magazine_home/crimjust_juvjus_cjstandards.html [May 2014].

Sickmund, M., Sladky, T.J., Kang, W., and Puzzanchera, C. (2011). *Easy Access to the Census of Juveniles in Residential Placement.* Washington, DC: Office of Juvenile Justice and Delinquency Prevention. Available: http://www.ojjdp.gov/ojstatbb/ezacjrp/ [July 2013].

Sickmund, M., Sladky, T.J., Kang, W., and Puzzanchera, C. (2013). *Easy Access to the Census of Juveniles in Residential Placement.* Washington, DC: Office of Juvenile Justice and Delinquency Prevention. Available: http://www.ojjdp.gov/ojstatbb/ezacjrp/ [July 2014].

Soler, M., Cocozza, J.J., and Henry, A. (2013). Providing and receiving technical assistance: Lessons learned from the field. In M. Soler, J. Cocozza, and A. Henry (Eds.), *MacArthur Foundation Models for Change* (pp. 10-15). Chicago, IL: Center for Children's Law and Policy and National Center for Mental Health and Juvenile Justice.

St. George, D. (2011). Judge Steve Teske seeks to keep kids with minor problems out of court. *Washington Post,* October 17, 2011. Available: http://www.washingtonpost.com/lifestyle/style/judge-steve-teske-seeks-to-keep-kids-with-minor-problems-out-of-court/2011/09/21/gIQA1y8ZsL_story.html [May 2014].

Steinberg, L., and Monahan, K.C. (2007). Age differences in resistance to peer influence. *Developmental Psychology, 43*(6), 1531-1543.

Steinberg, L., and Scott, E.S. (2003). Less guilty by reason of adolescence: Developmental immaturity, diminished responsibility, and the juvenile death penalty. *American Psychologist, 58*(12), 1009-1018.

Task Force on Community Preventive Services. (2007). Recommendation against policies facilitating the transfer of juveniles from juvenile to adult justice systems for the purpose of reducing violence. *American Journal of Preventive Medicine, 32*(4), 5-6.

Todnem, R. (2005). Organisational change management: A critical review. *Journal of Change Management, 5*(4), 369-380.

Trulson, C.R., Marquart, J.W., Mullings, J.L., and Caeti, T.J. (2007). In between adolescence and adulthood: Recidivism outcomes for a cohort of state delinquents. *Youth Violence and Juvenile Justice, 3*, 355-377.

U.S. Department of Education. (2014). *Data Snapshot: School Discipline*. Civil rights data collection issue brief no. 1. Office for Civil Rights. Available: http://www2.ed.gov/about/offices/list/ocr/docs/crdc-discipline-snapshot.pdf [May 2014].

U.S. Department of Justice. (2004). *The Internal Effects of the Federal Bureau of Investigation's Reprioritization*. Office of the Inspector General, Audit Report 04-39, September. Available: http://www.justice.gov/oig/reports/FBI/a0439/ch1.htm [May 2014].

U.S. Department of Justice. (2009a, April). *Procedures Used by the Office of Juvenile Justice and Delinquency Prevention to Award Discretionary Grants in FY 2007*. Audit Report 09-24. April. Office of the Inspector General, U.S. Department of Justice. Available: http://www.justice.gov/oig/reports/OJP/a0924/final.pdf [July 2014].

U.S. Department of Justice (2009b, February). *Improving the Grant Management Process*. Office of the Inspector General, U.S. Department of Justice. Available: http://www.justice.gov/oig/special/s0903/final.pdf [August 2014].

U.S. General Accounting Office. (2003, June). *FBI Reorganization: Progress Made in Efforts to Transform, but Major Challenges Continue*. GAO-03-759T. Washington, DC: U.S. Government Printing Office. Available: http://www.gao.gov/assets/120/110065.pdf [June 2014].

U.S. Government Accountability Office. (2005). *Practices That Can Help Enhance and Sustain Collaboration among Federal Agencies*. GAO-06-15. Available: http://www.gao.gov/assets/250/248219.pdf [May 2014].

U.S. Government Accountability Office. (2012, September). *Managing for Results: Key Considerations for Implementing Interagency Collaborative Mechanisms*. GAO-12-1022. Available: http://www.gao.gov/assets/650/648934.pdf [May 2014].

W. Haywood Burns Institute for Juvenile Justice Fairness & Equity. (2013). *Unbalanced Juvenile Justice*. Oakland, CA: W. Haywood Burns Institute. Available: http://data.burnsinstitute.org/about [May 2014].

Warwick, D.P. (1975). *A Theory of Public Bureaucracy*. Cambridge, MA: Harvard University Press.

Wasserman, G., Ko, S., and McReynolds, L. (2004). *Assessing the Mental Health Status of Youth in Juvenile Justice Settings*. Bulletin. Washington, DC: U.S. Department of Justice, Office of Justice Programs, Office of Juvenile Justice and Delinquency Prevention.

Wenger, E., McDermott, R., Snyder, W.M. (2002). *Cultivating Communities of Practice*. Cambridge: Harvard Business School Press.

Wiggins, L. (2008/2009). Managing the ups and downs of change communication. *Strategic Communication Management, 13*(1), 20-23.

Ziedenberg, J. (2014). *Case Study: New York City Department of Probation's Federal Partnership Efforts: Profile of a Successful Technical Assistance Collaboration with the Bureau of Justice Assistance and the National Institute of Corrections*. Washington, DC: Office of Justice Programs, Bureau of Justice Assistance and Bureau of Prisons, National Institute of Corrections.

Appendixes

Appendix A

Speakers and Interviews

SPEAKERS
FIRST COMMITTEE MEETING, JANUARY 21-22, 2014

TUESDAY, JANUARY 21, 2014
Washington, D.C.

2:15 p.m.   **Committee Charge and Sponsor Expectations for Study**
- Robert Listenbee Jr., *Administrator*, Office of Juvenile Justice and Delinquency Prevention, U.S. Department of Justice

- Laurie R. Garduque, *Director, Justice Reform*
  MacArthur Foundation

- Bart Lubow, *Director*
  Annie E. Casey Foundation

WEDNESDAY, January 22, 2014

8:30 a.m.   **Overview of OJJDP's Mission and Budget**
- Robert Listenbee Jr., *Administrator*, Office of Juvenile Justice and Delinquency Prevention, U.S. Department of Justice

- Janet Chiancone, *Associate Administrator, Budget and Administration Division*, Office of Juvenile Justice and Delinquency Prevention, U.S. Department of Justice

9:30 a.m.   **OJJDP Grant Making**
- Janet Chiancone, *Associate Administrator, Budget and Administration Division*, Office of Juvenile Justice and Delinquency Prevention, U.S. Department of Justice

10:45 a.m.   **Overview of OJJDP Training and Technical Assistance and Research**
- Brecht Donoghue, *Deputy Associate Administrator, Innovations and Research Division*,
  Office of Juvenile Justice and Delinquency Prevention
  U.S. Department of Justice

**SPEAKERS
SECOND COMMITTEE MEETING, FEBRUARY 13-14, 2014**

**THURSDAY, FEBRUARY 13, 2014
Washington, D.C.**

8:30 a.m.   **Panel—Legal System**
- Melissa Sickmund, *Director*
  National Center for Juvenile Justice
  National Council of Juvenile and Family Court Judges

- Susan Broderick, *Project Director*
  Center for Juvenile Justice Reform
  Georgetown University

- Mary Ann Scali, *Deputy Director*
  National Juvenile Defender Center

10:30 a.m.   **Presentation—State Advisory Groups**
- Marie Williams, *Executive Director*
  Coalition for Juvenile Justice

- Robin Jenkins, *Consultant*
  Coalition for Juvenile Justice

1:00 p.m.   **Panel—Family and Youth**
- Susan Badeau, *Speaker, Author and Trainer*

2:45 p.m.   **Panel—Racial and Ethnic Disparities**
- Alex Piquero, *Ashbel Smith Professor in Criminology*
  University of Texas at Dallas

- Bryan Sykes, *Assistant Professor of Sociology*
  DePaul University

FRIDAY, FEBRUARY 14, 2014

8:30 a.m.   **OJP Presentation and Discussion**
- Karol Mason, *Assistant Attorney General for the Office of Justice Programs*
  U.S. Department of Justice

10:00 a.m. **Panel—Advocacy**
- Carmen Daugherty, *Policy Director*
  Campaign for Youth Justice

- Sarah Bryer, *Director*
  National Juvenile Justice Network

- Marc Schindler, *Executive Director*
  Justice Policy Institute

SPEAKERS
THIRD COMMITTEE MEETING, MARCH 26-27, 2014

WEDNESDAY, MARCH 26, 2014
Washington, D.C.

8:30 a.m. **Panel—Perspectives on the Federal Role in
Reforming the Nation's Juvenile Justice System**
- Clarence J. Robinson
  Professor of Criminology, Law and Society
  George Mason University

- Mark Soler, *Executive Director*
  Center for Children's Law and Policy

10:15 a.m. **Panel—Perspectives from Judges and State Leaders of Reform**
- George Timberlake, *Judge* (ret.)
  Illinois Juvenile Justice Commission

- Dave Marsden, *Senator*
  State of Virginia

- Sarah Brown, *Program Director, Criminal Justice*
  National Conference of State Legislatures

- Juliana Stratton, *Executive Director*
  Cook County Justice Advisory Council

THURSDAY, MARCH 27, 2014

9:00 a.m. **Discussion—Juveniles Perspective**
- Brandon Jones, *Executive Director*
  New Generation Foundation

10:15 a.m. **Presentation—Racial and Ethnic Disparities (VTC)**
- Michael Finley, *Senior Program Associate*
  W. Haywood Burns Institute for Juvenile Justice, Fairness, and Equity

11:15 a.m. **Presentation—Data**
- Melissa Sickmund, *Director*
  National Center for Juvenile Justice

11:45 a.m. **Public and Sponsor Comments**
- Soledad McGrath, *Program Officer*
  MacArthur Foundation

- Carrie Rae Boatman, *Senior Policy Associate*
  Annie E. Casey Foundation

- Lyman Legters, *Casey Fellow*
  Office of Juvenile Justice and Delinquency Prevention
  U.S. Department of Justice

INTERVIEWS

Francis Mendez, Project Director, National Training and Technical Assistance Center: February 10, 2014

Shay Bilchik, Founder and Director, Center for Juvenile Justice Reform at Georgetown University's McCourt School of Public Policy: March 24, 2014

Gary Blau, Becky Flatow, and Kaitlyn Harrington, Substance Abuse and Mental Health Services Administration: April 7, 2014

Kathi Grasso and Robin Delany-Shabazz, Office of Juvenile Justice and Delinquency Prevention, current and former directors of the Coordinating Council on Juvenile Justice and Delinquency Prevention: April 11, 2014

Appendix B

The 2013 NRC Report in Brief

The 2013 National Research Council (NRC) report, *Reforming Juvenile Justice: A Developmental Approach*, by the Committee on Assessing Juvenile Justice Reform provided much of the research foundation for the work of the current study committee in preparing this report, *Implementing Juvenile Justice Reform: The Federal Role*. The "Report Brief" contained here was prepared by NRC staff within the Division of Behavioral and Social Sciences and Education to summarize the 2013 NRC report. In addition to capturing the key findings and recommendations of the 2013 NRC report, the brief outlines a set of guiding principles which offer actions that can be taken to achieve the goals of the juvenile justice system in a developmentally informed manner.

LAW AND JUSTICE

AT THE NATIONAL RESEARCH COUNCIL
www.nationalacademies.org/claj

REPORT BRIEF • NOVEMBER 2012

REFORMING JUVENILE JUSTICE:
A DEVELOPMENTAL APPROACH

The past decade has seen an explosion of knowledge about adolescent development and the neurobiological underpinnings of adolescent behavior. Much has also been learned about the pathways by which adolescents become delinquent, the effectiveness of prevention and treatment programs, and the long-term effects of transferring youths to the adult system and confining them in harsh conditions.

These findings have raised doubts about the wisdom and effectiveness of laws passed in the 1990s that criminalized many juvenile offenses and led more youths to be tried as adults. Some jurisdictions have already taken significant steps to reverse these policies and to overhaul their juvenile justice systems.

A new report from the National Research Council, *Reforming Juvenile Justice: A Developmental Approach,* aims to consolidate the progress that has been made in both science and policymaking and establish a strong platform for a 21st-century juvenile justice system. It takes an in-depth look at evidence on adolescent development and on effective responses to adolescent offending.

Changes are needed if the juvenile justice system is to meet its aims of holding adolescents accountable, preventing reoffending, and treating them fairly, the report concludes. It recommends that state and tribal governments review their laws and policies and align them with emerging evidence on adolescent development and effective interventions.

THE NATIONAL ACADEMIES
Advisers to the Nation on Science, Engineering, and Medicine

National Academy of Sciences • National Academy of Engineering • Institute of Medicine • National Research Council

EMERGING SCIENCE ON ADOLESCENCE

Falling between childhood and adulthood, adolescence is when a person develops an integrated sense of self, which includes separating from parents and developing an individual identity. As part of that process, adolescents often engage in novelty-seeking and risky behavior, such as alcohol and drug use, unsafe sex, and reckless driving.

Research has shown that adolescents differ from adults in at least three important ways that lead to differences in behavior:

- Adolescents are less able to regulate their own behavior in emotionally charged contexts.

- Adolescents are more sensitive to external influences such as peer pressure and immediate rewards.

- Adolescents show less ability to make judgments and decisions that require future orientation.

Evidence suggests that these cognitive tendencies are linked to the biological immaturity of the brain and an imbalance among developing brain systems. The brain system that influences pleasure-seeking and emotional reactivity develops more rapidly than the brain system that supports self-control, leaving adolescents less capable of self-regulation than adults. The likelihood and seriousness of offending are also strongly affected by influences in youths' environment — peers, parents, schools, and communities. In addition, perceived racial discrimination has been linked to antisocial behavior.

Research shows that, for most youths, the period of risky experimentation does not extend beyond adolescence, ceasing as identity settles with maturity. The vast majority of youths who are arrested or referred to juvenile court have not committed serious offenses, and half of them appear in the system only once. Evidence indicates that youths who commit serious offenses such as homicide, aggravated

WHO IS AN ADOLESCENT?

Scientifically, adolescence has no precise chronological onset or endpoint. It refers to a phase in development between childhood and adulthood beginning at puberty, typically about 12 or 13, and ending in the late teens or early twenties. Generally speaking, the committee's report focuses on those under age 18 and refers to this age group as juveniles — the term used in the legal system — or youths.

assault, and burglary are a very small proportion of the overall delinquent population, and that their behavior is driven by the same risk factors and developmental processes that influence other juvenile offenders.

THE EXISTING JUVENILE JUSTICE SYSTEM

In 2008, 28 percent of delinquency cases that were adjudicated resulted in youths being placed outside the home, such as in a group home or juvenile correctional facility. Confining youths away from their homes and communities interferes with three social conditions that contribute to adolescents' healthy psychological development:

- the presence of a parent or parent figure who is involved with the adolescent and concerned about his or her successful development;

- association with peers who value and model positive social behavior and academic success; and

- activities that require autonomous decision-making and critical thinking. Schools, extracurricular activities, and work settings can provide opportunities for adolescents to learn to think for themselves, develop self-reliance and self-efficacy, and improve reasoning skills.

In addition, many youths face collateral consequences of involvement in the justice system, such as the public release of juvenile records that follow them throughout their lives and limit future educational and employment opportunities.

These disadvantages are borne disproportionately by some groups of adolescents. Racial and ethnic minorities are overrepresented at every stage of the juvenile justice system; they are more likely to be arrested, and, for certain offenses, more likely to face harsh punishment. They also remain in the system longer than white youths. Adolescents who move between the child welfare and juvenile justice systems, and those with mental health disorders, are also more likely to be treated harshly.

A DEVELOPMENTAL APPROACH TO JUVENILE JUSTICE

The overarching goal of the juvenile justice system is to support the positive social development of youths who become involved in the system, and thereby assure the safety of communities. The specific aims of juvenile courts and affiliated agencies are to hold youths accountable for wrongdoing, prevent further offending, and treat youths fairly. All three of these aims are compatible with a developmental approach to juvenile justice.

Accountability. Holding adolescents accountable for their offenses aims to ensure that offenders will be answerable for wrongdoing, particularly for conduct that causes harm to identifiable victims. It does not follow, however, that the mechanisms of accountability for juveniles should mimic adult punishments. Condemnation, control, and lengthy confinement ("serving time") — the identifying attributes of criminal punishment — are not ordinarily needed to assure that juveniles are held accountable. Juvenile courts should provide an opportunity for youths to accept responsibility for their actions, make amends to individual victims and the community, and participate in community service or other kinds of programs. Examples of appropriate approaches include restorative justice programs that involve victims and adjudication programs that involve restitution and peers.

Preventing reoffending. Whether a juvenile court can reduce reoffending depends on its ability to intervene with the right adolescent offenders and use the right type of intervention. The first step in enabling courts to do this is by implementing risk and need assessments. Risk assessments gauge whether a youth is at low, medium, or high risk of reoffending based on factors such as prior offending history and school performance. Newer instruments also assess the youth's needs, acknowledging that the risk of reoffending is not a fixed attribute but an estimate that might be lowered by particular interventions, monitoring in the community, or changes in life situation. Using these tools can allow resources to be better targeted, focusing the more intense and costly interventions on those at greater risk of reoffending.

If implemented well, evidence-based interventions — for example, certain types of therapy, such as aggression replacement therapy and cognitive-behavioral therapy — reduce reoffending and produce remarkably large economic returns relative to their costs. In general, community-based interventions show greater reductions in rearrests than programs offered in institutional settings. Once in institutional care, adequate time — arguably up to about six months — is needed to provide sufficiently intense services for adolescents to benefit. There is no convincing evidence, however, that confinement of juvenile offenders beyond the minimum amount needed for this purpose appreciably reduces the likelihood of subsequent offending.

Fairness. Treating youths fairly and with dignity can enhance moral development and legal socialization during adolescence. The juvenile court should assure that youths are represented by properly trained counsel and have an opportunity to participate in the proceedings. However, lawyers in juvenile courts often have too few resources and are overburdened by high caseloads.

GUIDING PRINCIPLES FOR JUVENILE JUSTICE REFORM

ACCOUNTABILITY

- Use the justice system to communicate the message that society expects youths to take responsibility for their actions and the foreseeable consequences of their actions.

- Encourage youths to accept responsibility for admitted or proven wrongdoing, consistent with protecting their legal rights.

- Facilitate constructive involvement of family members in the proceedings to assist youths to accept responsibility and carry out the obligations set by the court.

- Use restitution and community service as instruments of accountability to victims and the community.

- Use confinement sparingly and only when needed to respond to and prevent serious reoffending.

- Avoid collateral consequences of adjudication such as public release of juvenile records that reduce opportunities for a successful transition to a prosocial adult life.

PREVENTING REOFFENDING

- Use structured risk and need assessment instruments to identify low-risk youths who can be handled less formally in community-based settings, to match youths with specialized treatment, and to target more intensive and expensive interventions toward high-risk youths.

- Use clearly specified interventions rooted in knowledge about adolescent development and tailored to the particular adolescent's needs and social environment.

- Engage the adolescent's family as much as possible and draw on neighborhood resources to foster positive activities, prosocial development, and law-abiding behavior.

- Eliminate interventions that rigorous evaluation research has shown to be ineffective or harmful.

- Keep accurate data on the type and intensity of interventions provided and the results achieved.

FAIRNESS

- Ensure that youths are represented throughout the process by properly trained counsel unless the right is voluntarily and intelligently waived by the youth.

- Ensure that youths are adjudicated only if they are competent to understand the proceedings and assist counsel.

- Facilitate participation by youths in all proceedings.

- Intensify efforts to reduce racial and ethnic disparities, as well as other patterns of unequal treatment, in the administration of juvenile justice.

- Ensure that youths perceive that they have been treated fairly and with dignity.

- Establish and implement evidence-based measures for fairness based on both legal criteria and perceptions of youths, families, and other participants.

To improve the quality of representation and enhance youths' perception of justice, states should clarify the obligations of juvenile defense counsel at every stage of the case and should specify caseload limits in accordance with recommended standards.

A critical aspect of achieving a fair juvenile justice system is reducing racial and ethnic disparities. Several interventions and policy initiatives have been undertaken to reduce disparities, but there is little scientific evidence on whether they are effective. Federal, state, and local governments should intensify their efforts to address disparities in a focused and transparent manner.

ROLE OF THE OFFICE OF JUVENILE JUSTICE AND DELINQUENCY PREVENTION (OJJDP)

The juvenile justice field is moving toward a more developmentally appropriate system, with states and local jurisdictions taking the lead as federal dollars have waned. But the need for technical assistance and training is critical. Historically, such assistance has come from the Office of Juvenile Justice and Delinquency Prevention (OJJDP) in the Department of Justice. Congress established this office in 1974, giving it a broad mandate to develop and disseminate knowledge to the juvenile justice field, assist states and local jurisdictions in improving their juvenile justice systems, develop national standards, and coordinate federal activities related to the treatment of juvenile offenders. Unfortunately, OJJDP's capacity to carry out this mandate has dramatically declined over the past decade, in part due to inadequate funding and a severe restriction of its discretion in determining how its resources should be used.

RECOMMENDATIONS

The committee made recommendations for a developmentally informed juvenile justice system and for incorporating new evidence into policy and practice on a continuing basis.

Given current realities regarding the role of OJJDP and the role of the federal government in general, the immediate momentum for change will continue to come from the state, local, and tribal jurisdictions.

Among the committee's recommendations:

State and tribal governments should establish bipartisan multistakeholder task forces or commissions under the auspices of the governor or tribal leader, the legislature, or the highest state court to undertake a thorough and transparent assessment of their juvenile justice systems. They should align their laws, policies and practices with evolving knowledge about adolescent development and evidence-based programs. In addition, they should intensify efforts to identify and eliminate policies that tend to disadvantage minorities, to publicly report on the scope of the problem, and to evaluate programs aimed at reducing disparities.

Federal policymakers should restore OJJDP's capacity to carry out its core mission through reauthorization, appropriations, and funding flexibility. OJJDP has been effective in the past in spearheading major reforms that reflect key developmental principles: keeping youths separated from adult offenders, addressing racial disparities, and avoiding unnecessary detention for youths. These protections need to be strengthened by:

- defining status offenses to include offenses such as possession of alcohol or tobacco that apply only to youths under 21.

- removing all exceptions to the detention of youths who commit offenses that would not be punishable by confinement if committed by an adult. For example, a youth should not be confined for an offense such as truancy or running away.

- modifying the definition of an "adult inmate" to give states flexibility to keep youths in juvenile facilities until they reach the age of extended juvenile court jurisdiction.

- expanding the protections to all youths under 18 in pretrial detention, whether they are charged in juvenile or adult courts.

In addition, OJJDP should prioritize its research, training, and technical assistance resources to promote the adoption of developmentally appropriate policies and practices and expand the number of jurisdictions actively engaged in activities to reduce racial disparities.

Federal research agencies, such as the National Science Foundation, Centers for Disease Control and Prevention, and National Institutes of Health, as well as OJJDP, should support research that continues to advance the science of adolescent development, expanding our understanding of the ways developmental processes influence juvenile delinquency and how the juvenile justice system should respond.

The Bureau of Justice Statistics and other government and private statistical agencies should, under OJJDP's leadership, develop a data improvement program on juvenile offending and juvenile justice system processing that provides greater insight into state and local variations. At the state and local level, data should be collected on the gender, age, race and ethnicity of offenders as well as offense charged or committed; arrest, detention, and disposition practices; and recidivism.

COMMITTEE ON ASSESSING JUVENILE JUSTICE REFORM

ROBERT L. JOHNSON (Chair), University of Medicine and Dentistry, New Jersey Medical School; **RICHARD J. BONNIE** (Vice-Chair), *IOM Member*, University of Virginia; **CARL C. BELL**, Community Mental Health Council, Inc.; **LAWRENCE D. BOBO**, *NAS Member*, Harvard University; **JEFFREY A. BUTTS**, John Jay College of Criminal Justice; **GLADYS CARRIÓN**, New York State Office of Children & Family Service; **B.J. CASEY,** Weill Medical College of Cornell University; **KENNETH A. DODGE**, Duke University; **SANDRA A. GRAHAM**, University of California, Los Angeles; **ERNESTINE GRAY**, Orleans Parish Juvenile Court, New Orleans, Louisiana; **EDWARD P. MULVEY**, University of Pittsburgh School of Medicine; **ROBERT PLOTNICK,** University of Washington; **ELIZABETH S. SCOTT**, Columbia University; **TERENCE P. THORNBERRY**, University of Maryland, College Park; **CHERIE TOWNSEND**, Texas Department of Juvenile Justice; **BETTY M. CHEMERS**, *Study Director*

FOR MORE INFORMATION...This brief was prepared by the Committee on Law and Justice based on the report *Reforming Juvenile Justice: A Developmental Approach.* The study was sponsored by the Office of Juvenile Justice and Delinquency Prevention. Any opinions, findings, conclusions, or recommendations expressed in this publication are those of the authors and do not reflect those of the sponsor. Copies of the report are available from the National Academies Press, 500 Fifth Street, N.W., Washington, DC 20001; (800) 624-6242; http://www.nap.edu.

THE NATIONAL ACADEMIES
Advisers to the Nation on Science, Engineering, and Medicine

The nation turns to the National Academies—National Academy of Sciences, National Academy of Engineering, Institute of Medicine, and National Research Council—for independent, objective advice on issues that affect people's lives worldwide.
www.national-academies.org

Appendix C

Committee Biographies

Richard J. Bonnie (IOM) (chair) is the Harrison Foundation professor of medicine and law, professor of psychiatry and neurobehavioral sciences, professor of public policy, and director, Institute of Law, Psychiatry and Public Policy at the University of Virginia. He was elected to the Institute of Medicine (IOM) in 1991. He teaches and writes about criminal law, bioethics, and public policies relating to mental health, substance abuse, aging, and public health. He was associate director of the National Commission on Marijuana and Drug Abuse, secretary of the first National Advisory Council on Drug Abuse, and chief adviser for the American Bar Association's Criminal Justice Mental Health Standards Project. He chaired the Virginia Commission on Mental Health Law Reform. He served on the MacArthur Foundation's Research Networks on Mental Health and the Law and Mandated Community Treatment and is currently serving on the Network on Law and Neuroscience. He received the Yarmolinsky Medal in 2002 for contributions to IOM and the National Academies. In 2007, Bonnie received the University of Virginia's highest honor, the Thomas Jefferson Award. He has a B.A. from Johns Hopkins University and an LL.B. from the University of Virginia School of Law.

Sam Abed is the secretary of Maryland's Department of Juvenile Services. Previously he served as deputy director of operations at the Virginia Department of Juvenile Justice, with direct supervision over juvenile justice operations, including the supervision of 6 juvenile correctional facilities and 32 court service units statewide. Previously, he served as assistant commonwealth attorney for the Office of the Sussex County Commonwealth's Attorney and for the Office of the City of Norfolk Commonwealth's Attorney. He also served as commissioner for the Virginia Commission for National and Community Service. Mr. Abed received a B.S. in psychology from the Virginia Polytechnic Institute and State University and completed an internship at the American University in Cairo, Arabic Language Institute. He received his J.D. from the University of Richmond School of Law.

Grace Bauer is the executive director of Justice for Families, a national alliance of local organizations founded and run by parents and families who have experienced the juvenile justice system directly with their own children and who are taking the lead to help build a family-driven and trauma-informed youth justice system. Previously, she helped organize parents to form the Lake Charles chapter of Families and Friends of Louisiana's Incarcerated Children (FFLIC). Rapidly recruiting and training new members and increasing FFLIC's visibility and influence, the chapter became an integral part of the passage of the Louisiana Juvenile Justice Reform Act of 2003 and the closing of the infamous Tallulah juvenile prison. She joined the Campaign for Youth Justice in 2008, where she united parents and allies of children in six targeted states to change laws and practices prosecuting and confining children as adults. She also led the development of the National Parent Caucus, a national network of family members seeking to end the practice of trying, sentencing, and incarcerating children as adults.

Kevin J. Bethel is presently in charge of Patrol Operations for the Philadelphia Police Department, where he oversees both the patrol and detective units for the entire city of Philadelphia. Since completion of the Police Academy in 1986, his assignments have included: police officer-6th District; sergeant-17th District; sergeant-Special Investigative Bureau, Narcotics Strike Force; sergeant-Special Investigative Bureau, Narcotics Field Unit, North Central section; lieutenant-18th District; lieutenant-Internal Affairs Division and lieutenant-Narcotics Intelligence Investigative Unit. Prior to his appointment as deputy commissioner, he served as the commanding officer (captain) of the 17th Police District from 2005 to 2008. He serves on the Advisory Board to the initiative, by the International Association of Chiefs of Police and the MacArthur Foundation, on "Law Enforcement's Leadership Role in the Advancement of Promising Practices in Juvenile Justice." Deputy Commissioner Bethel holds a B.S. in criminal justice from Chestnut Hill College and an M.A. in public safety from St. Joseph's University.

Sandra A. Graham is a professor of psychological studies in education and chair of the Department of Education at University of California, Los Angeles (UCLA). She received her Ph.D. in education at UCLA. Dr. Graham's teaching interests include achievement motivation, attribution theory, motivation in minority groups, social development, adolescent development, risk, and resiliency. Her research interests are in the areas of cognitive approaches to motivation, the development of attributional processes, motivation in African Americans, and peer-directed aggression and victimization. Dr. Graham is currently principal investigator on grants from the National Science Foundation and the W. T. Grant Foundation. She also is the recipient of an Independent Scientist Award, funded by the National Institute of Mental Health. She is a former recipient of the Early Contribution Award from Division 15 (Educational Psychology) of the American Psychological Association and a former fellow at the Center for Advanced Study in the Behavioral Sciences, Stanford, California. She is an associate editor of *Developmental Psychology* and a member of the MacArthur Foundation Network on Adolescent Development and Juvenile Justice.

Maxwell Griffin, Jr., was appointed associate judge in the Circuit Court of Cook County in 2003. He currently serves in the Child Protection Division of the Cook County Juvenile Court. Judge Griffin joined the bench after a 22-year career as an attorney, during which he received peer recognition in 2003 from *Chicago Lawyer* as one of the top 20 tort defense lawyers in Chicago. He served as assistant state's attorney in the Civil Actions Bureau as well as a plaintiff's personal injury lawyer. Judge Griffin is a member of the Board of Trustees of the National Council of Juvenile and Family Court Judges and a board member for the Illinois Judicial Association. He serves as co-lead judge for the Chicago Model Juvenile Court. He is an adjunct faculty member at IIT Chicago-Kent College of Law and is a member of the Administrative Office of the Illinois Courts' education faculty. He is the author of a chapter on medical and mental rights of minors in the Illinois Institute for Continuing Legal Education's *Juvenile Law Handbook*. Judge Griffin is a 1980 graduate of the University of Notre Dame Law School.

Patricia Lee has served as a deputy public defender in San Francisco since 1978 and has practiced in the juvenile courts since 1981. She is currently the managing attorney of the San Francisco Public Defender's juvenile office, and co-director of the Pacific Juvenile Defender Center, which seeks to improve the quality of representation provided by juvenile delinquency attorneys. She served as a technical adviser to the American Bar Association Office of Juvenile Justice and Delinquency Prevention for the Due Process Advocacy Program, which seeks to increase children's access to quality counsel in juvenile delinquency proceedings. She also established the country's first advocacy program for girls who have been victims of exploitation. She is a member of the MacArthur Foundation's Network on Adolescent Development and Juvenile Justice and a member of the Family and Juvenile Law Advisory Committee of the Administrative Office of the Courts, Center for Families, Children and the Courts. She received her undergraduate degree from the University of California, Berkeley, and a law degree from Lincoln University School of Law.

Edward P. Mulvey is professor of psychiatry and director of the Law and Psychiatry Program at the Western Psychiatric Institute and Clinic at the University of Pittsburgh's School of Medicine. His research has focused on issues related to how clinicians make judgments regarding the type of risk posed by adult mental patients and the development and treatment of serious juvenile offenders. He is a fellow of the American Psychological Association and the American Psychological Society, a recipient of a faculty scholar's award from the William T. Grant Foundation, a member of two MacArthur Foundation Research Networks (one on mental health and the law and another on adolescent development and juvenile justice), and a member of the Steering Committee of the National Consortium on Violence Research. He currently serves on the Science Advisory Board of the Office of Justice Programs of the U.S. Department of Justice. He has a Ph.D. in community/clinical psychology from the University of Virginia. He also did postdoctoral training in quantitative methods in criminal justice at Carnegie Mellon University.

Alex R. Piquero is Ashbel Smith professor of criminology in the School of Economic, Political, and Policy Sciences at the University of Texas at Dallas; adjunct professor at the Key Centre for Ethics, Law, Justice, and Governance, Griffith University; and co-editor of the *Journal of Quantitative Criminology*. He has published over 200 peer-reviewed articles in the areas of criminal careers, criminological theory, and quantitative research methods and has collaborated on several books. In addition to his membership on over a dozen editorial boards of journals in criminology and sociology, he has also served as executive counselor with the American Society of Criminology, member of the National Academy of Sciences Panel Evaluating the National Institute of Justice, member of the Racial Democracy, Crime and Justice Network at Ohio State University, and member of the MacArthur Foundation's Research Network on Adolescent Development and Juvenile Justice.

Vincent Schiraldi is a senior adviser for the New York City Mayor's Office of Criminal Justice. From his appointment in February 2010 until March 2014, Schiraldi served as commissioner of the New York City Department of Probation, bringing 30 years of experience working with troubled youth and juvenile justice systems. Prior to 2010, he served as the District of Columbia's first director of the Department of Youth Rehabilitation Services, where he launched major reforms. He has served as an adviser on the Washington, DC, Blue Ribbon Commission on Youth Safety and Juvenile Justice Reform, as a member of the California Blue Ribbon Commission on Inmate Population Management, as an advisor to the California Commission on the Status of African American Men; and as the first chair of the San Francisco Juvenile Probation Commission. He has published numerous papers and articles and has spoken before a variety of academic and governmental audiences. He received his M.S.W. from New York University and holds a B.A. in social psychology from Binghamton University in Binghamton, New York.

Cherie Townsend is currently an independent consultant and executive coach for individuals and organizations. She has nearly 40 years of experience as a juvenile justice practitioner and leader, serving as executive director of the Texas Department of Juvenile Justice and the Texas Youth Commission. She led staff in these agencies in a reform effort that dramatically improved outcomes while also closing six secure facilities and eliminating 2,000 staff positions. The reform effort resulted in facilities receiving American Correctional Association accreditation and participating in performance-based standards data collection to target continuous improvement, engagement of families, expanded specialized treatment, and investment in prevention and re-entry services. She also served as director of juvenile justice services in Clark County, Nevada (Las Vegas), a Juvenile Detention Alternatives Initiative replication site, and as director of juvenile court services in Maricopa County, Arizona (Phoenix). She received the George M. Keiser Award for Exceptional Leadership and has been recognized by the Texas Corrections Association, the Council of Juvenile Correctional Administrators, the National Juvenile Court Services Association, and the National Association of Probation Executives. She is a member of the Suicide Prevention Resource Center Steering Committee and the National Re-entry Resource Center Advisory Committee on Juvenile Justice. She has an M.P.A. from Southern Methodist University and an M.B.A. from the University of Texas.

John A. Tuell is the executive director of the Robert F. Kennedy National Resource Center for Juvenile Justice at the Robert F. Kennedy Children's Action Corps. Prior to this appointment, he served as the director of the MacArthur

Foundation Models for Change Initiative at the Robert F. Kennedy Children's Action Corps. From 2009 to 2013, Mr. Tuell served as the president of Tuell and Associates Consultation, LLC, which provided expert consultation and technical assistance in juvenile justice, child welfare, and multisystem reform and quality improvements. He has authored or contributed to numerous publications and issue briefs supporting the Child Welfare-Juvenile Justice Systems Integration Initiative and addressing other issues relevant to the juvenile justice system. He served in the U.S. Department of Justice as deputy director of the State Relations and Assistance Division in OJJDP. He provided managerial oversight to grant management staff overseeing six grant programs; the Comprehensive Strategy for Serious, Chronic, and Violent Offenders Initiative; and for the Juvenile Accountability Incentive Block Grant Program. From 1979 to 1997, he worked in the Fairfax County, Virginia, Juvenile and Domestic Relations District Court as a probation officer, field office probation supervisor, and intake officer and as an administrator at a residential treatment facility for serious and chronic juvenile offenders. Hel earned his B.S.W. from James Madison University and his M.A. in criminal justice from George Washington University.